ONLY CLOSERS MAKE BIG MONEY

By David Plummer

ONLY CLOSERS make BIG MONEY

By David E. Plummer

Copyright © 1999
by
David E. Plummer

Published by
Historical Publications, Inc.
8030 North MoPac
Suite #305
Austin, Texas 78759

ISBN # 1-881825-24-8

Editing/Arrangement by Nancy Crumpton
Cover Design by Jeffrey Breckenridge/Ellis Graphics, Inc.
Book Design/Typesetting by - David Nielsen/PC Bits & Bytes

Printed in The United States of America by Armstrong Printing
using
www.printandbind.com

ACKNOWLEDGMENT

This book is dedicated to my wife, Jody,
and our children, Jamie, Roger, and Linzi.
I want to thank them for their patience and understanding during the
many times I was on the road pursuing my career.

I want to thank Mark. J. McDonnell,
my best friend and business partner, whose ability to
maintain a positive attitude in spite of personal tragedies
is an inspiration to me.

I also want to thank my deceased uncle,
Roy E. McAfee, who taught me to treat everyone the way
I wish to be treated. His bottom line was
"what goes around, comes around."

Finally, I want to thank my brother,
Dapper Dan, whose "mind over matter" attitude towards
Life has influenced me immeasurably.

INTRODUCTION

This book is about making sales—more specifically, it's about *closing* sales. Whether you're new to the sales profession or a veteran salesperson, you already know that closing is the most crucial part of the sales process. Regardless of how polished your presentation is or how charming your personality, they mean nothing if you don't close the sale. My purpose in writing this book is to impart my knowledge, gleaned from 25 years of experience and from listening to people whom I found to be inspirational, about the *science* of closing.

Customers come up with all kinds of objections to closing a sale. In this book I provide detailed instructions on how to completely overcome any objection from "I'll think it over" to "I can't afford it." I have developed meaningful and concise responses to these objections that are designed to motivate the customer to close the sale. In most cases money is the real reason behind an objection, and this book gives instructions on how to determine what the real objection is and how to overcome it. You'll also learn how to get your customers to verbalize their objections so that you can deal with them. After all, if you don't know what's preventing a customer from closing, you can't address their objections. I also provide examples of realistic, everyday situations I have encountered in my career. These are situations that any salesperson encounters sooner or later, and you'll find it helps to know in advance what to expect and how you can help customers make sound decisions. And at some point you have to know when to quit talking and start closing. This book is an educational tool that provides detailed information about the entire process of making a sale, from the presentation to the close. If you're willing to learn the techniques it takes to close sales, this book can be the key to a successful career.

I developed the information in this book through 25 years of sales experience, which includes 15 years of training salespeople. In addition, I have been motivated and inspired by such renown authors and speakers as Zig Ziglar, Tom Hopkins, and Ben Gay III. From them and my personal experience, I've learned that a successful salesperson must be willing to do what it takes to stay motivated. I've read books and listened to hours and hours of tapes. This book contains the information I've learned from these books, tapes, and speakers, and through my own relentless desire to succeed. This is information that I've compiled and condensed into powerful techniques for closing sales.

The topics covered in the chapters can help even a veteran salesperson. In Chapter 2, "Salespeople," I describe what distinguishes a great closer (a great salesperson) from an ordinary salesperson. In Part 2, I discuss the elements of an effective presentation, and how you can turn objections around to actually help you close the sale. In Part 3, I discuss the various closes you can use, which include the Columbo Sharp Angle close, Lost Opportunity close, and Bring Back the Hamburger Close.

Let's take a frequently heard objection, "I can't afford it," and apply the principles of the science of closing to learn how to close the sale after having heard this objection. If customers make this objection, it means they need more information. Saying "I can't afford it," means they *can* afford it if the financing is adjusted to meet their needs. You need to find out if it's the initial investment that they can't afford, and if so, you focus on that and adjust it to a level they can afford. If they say it's the monthly investment they can't afford, focus on that payment.

When money is the obstacle, you can usually work it out if you approach it skillfully. Suppose the customer says it's neither the initial investment nor the monthly investment but the total cost that is unaffordable. You can ask questions that will reveal the dollar amount the customer is willing to spend, and you can use this information to adjust the cost of the product, if it can be adjusted, or offer an alternative product that is affordable to close the sale.

If you know how to respond to a customer's objections, you can close the sale. This book describes every imaginable objection and how you should respond.

The example provided here is just one of many that are described in this book. A glossary of terms is also included. Sales is the highest paying profession in the world, and by reading this book you can become a master at the science of closing. If you want to stay challenged and motivated in your work, if you want to increase your income, and if you want to challenge and motivate your own sales force, read on.

TABLE OF CONTENTS

Acknowledgment v

Introduction vii

Part 1: What It Takes
Chapter 1: Desire 3
Chapter 2: Salespeople 11

Part 2: The Presentation
Chapter 3: Tools of the Trade 23
Chapter 4: Elements of an Effective Presentation . . .33
Chapter 5: Downselling 49
Chapter 6: Rescissions and Manageritis 53
Chapter 7: Using Tie-Downs 59
Chapter 8: Handling Objections 63

Part 3: The Close
Chapter 9: Introductory Closes 69
Chapter 10: Sharp Angle Closes 79
Chapter 11: Bring Back the Hamburger Close 87
Chapter 12: Verbal Ben Close 93
Chapter 13: One Day Closes 103
Chapter 14: Money Closes 119
Chapter 15: In Summary 137

Glossary: The Great Salesperson's Vocabulary 143

Part 1: What It Takes

No one said life was going to be easy.
—"Dapper" Dan Plummer

1

DESIRE

Sales is a high paying profession; in fact, some would say it is the highest paying profession. At the beginning of my sales career, I asked myself why this was true, and as my sales career took off, I finally figured out the answer. It's because salespeople of any age can determine their income. They earn as much as they sell; it's as simple as that.

Sales is the most gratifying of all professions. In what other profession than sales is the sky the limit regarding income? People are more afraid to go into sales than any other type of work because they think there is no security in sales. And to those people, I ask one question: since no job is secure, do you want to work in a field where your income is limited or in one where the sky is the limit? Notice the word *limit* in the previous sentence. The fact of the matter is the only limit is one you put on yourself. Negative thoughts can limit you as much as positive thoughts can *un-limit* you.

There is no substitute for positive thinking and self-motivation in the profession of selling. I am not saying a person has to be on a high all the time because that's not possible. What I am saying is you cannot be thinking of what happened yesterday. There is a club designed for people who dwell on the past. It is called the "If-I-Could've-Club"; it's also known as 20/20 hindsight.

Many years ago, my best friend and business partner, Mark J. McDonnell, told me four beliefs that I remember on a daily basis, which apply to the sales profession:

1. There is no such thing as a free lunch.
2. There is no substitute for good hard work.
3. You only get out of life what you are willing to put into it.
4. What happens, happens for the best.

Many people who are not successful in sales make excuses for their failure—excuses such as, "I cannot put pressure on people to make decisions" and "It's not fair to push people." What these people are really saying is that they are not willing to learn the techniques required to help people make sound decisions. These excuses are made to cover up the fact that these people are just not willing to do what it takes to succeed.

Great athletes succeed because they train harder than others. Top executives are willing to put in more time and effort than others; skilled mechanics go to continuing education classes to keep up with changes and new designs. It is the same in any profession: you have to be willing to do what it takes.

Roger Staubach and David Robinson have both achieved great success in sports. Both attended the Naval Academy, and both are great athletes. Robert Staubach won the coveted Heisman Trophy for being the best college football player his senior year. Both were drafted by professional teams, but because they had to honor their commitment to the Navy, they did not go into pro ball the year following their graduation. They continued training, though, so they would be prepared for professional sports. They had to train harder, longer, and with more desire if they were to make it as pros. You can never train too hard or learn too much.

After a full day of sales calls, it's tough to get as psyched up for the last call as you were for the first one. My secret is simple: tell yourself, "I am tired and do not feel like giving this presentation." Then say, "I need to kick myself into high gear." This gives you a mental boost. If you do not psyche yourself up, you might as well go home. Do not give the presentation because it will be a waste of your prospect's time.

Do not just go through the motions and hope you will sell something. Do not take short cuts. Challenge yourself mentally. Get ready and get charged. It will definitely increase your paycheck.

You have to have a strong will to be successful in the sales world. A good friend of mine, Karl Johnson, came to work one morning looking tired. I asked him what was wrong, and he told me he did not get much sleep the night before. I challenged him by asking, "You are going to sell something today. Aren't you?" He looked at me, smiled, and said, "Don't I always?" and I couldn't deny it. He is truly one of the best salespersons I have ever known. He told me because he felt bad, it made him try harder. The pros know when the going gets tough, the tough make sales. They are aware of the hills and valleys but keep producing because they are always prepared and their will is strong.

True closers are always looking for ways to better themselves professionally. They constantly read, study, and learn new information, sometimes reading the same book several times. They listen to tapes on sales and motivation. Always willing to get more sales training, they go to seminars whenever possible. They use the information they learn from these seminars to sell their products. True closers realize knowledge is power, and the more power they have, the more success they will have in the sales profession.

Great salespeople strive to improve their situation by always reaching for higher goals, higher incomes, and a better quality of life for themselves and their families. There is nothing wrong with wanting material things for you and your family. To reach these goals you have to have a relentless desire to succeed. Many salespeople never reach their potential because they are not willing to learn new techniques and styles, which is death in the sales profession. If you fall in this category, *get out* of this profession, or you will eventually be driven out. Reading books and listening to tapes are the best ways I know to stay motivated.

Earlier in this chapter I suggested that the sales profession is perhaps the highest paying occupation in the world. The only person who can limit your income is yourself. Even though most salespeople realize this fact, some still are content to be in the 80 percent who make only 20 percent of all sales. They *themselves* and only *themselves* are responsible for their being in this cellar. They will not elevate themselves to the 20 percent who make 80 percent of all the sales because they do not do what it takes to be a great salesperson.

If you feel you are on the cellar team, or in this 80 percentile who make only 20 percent of the sales, answer these questions. Prior to reading this book, when was the last time you read a book about sales? Do you have any sales tapes you listen to on the way to and from work? When was the last sales seminar you attended? Your answers to these questions can reveal why you're not making the salary you want.

Are you one of those salespeople who have been doing this for twenty years and think you know it all? If so, write this down, and read it back to yourself: *old salespeople never die, they just lose their commissions.* That is exactly what happens! Do you write down certain points about your product and implement this information in your sales presentation? Do you try to learn from people who come from all walks of life?

Great salespeople know they can learn from anyone, not just successful salespeople. Constantly implementing new ideas, they observe and listen to everyone around them. By listening, they can pick up and use amazing tidbits of information. The sum total of little ideas makes for great ones. Listen and use them.

Let me tell you a story I once read. A young man was caught up in "gold fever" during the gold rush days. He decided to travel west to dig for gold and grow rich. He never heard that more gold has been mined from the thoughts of men than has ever been taken from the earth. He staked a claim and went to work laboring day and night.

After weeks of hard work, he was rewarded by the discovery of shining ore. Needing machinery to bring the ore to the surface, he covered up the mine and returned home. He proceeded to tell his relatives and neighbors about the strike. They got together and raised the money for the needed machinery. He then journeyed back to the mine field, and the first car of ore was mined and shipped to a smelter. It proved that he had one of the richest mines in the state. A few more cars of ore would clear all his debts, and after that he would be rolling in money. Down went the drills and up went the hope. Then all of a sudden the vein of ore disappeared. He had come to the end of the rainbow, and the pot of gold was no longer there. He desperately tried to pick up the vein again, all to no avail. Finally, he decided to quit.

He sold the machinery to a junk man for three hundred dollars and took the train back home. The junk man called a friend who was a mining engineer and asked him to make some calculations. The engineer advised that the project had failed because the previous owner was not familiar with fault lines. His calculations showed that the vein would be found just three feet from where the young man had stopped drilling. That is exactly where it was found. The junk man took millions of dollars more from the mine because he sought expertise *before giving up*.

Long afterward the young man recouped his loss many times over when he made the discovery that *desire* can be transmitted into gold. The discovery came after he went into the business of life insurance. Remembering that he lost a huge fortune because he stopped three feet from gold, he profited from that previous experience in his new profession by saying to himself, "I stopped three feet from gold once, but I will never stop because men say 'no' when I ask them to buy insurance." He became one of a small group who sold over a million dollars of life insurance annually. He owed his "stickability" to the lesson learned from quitting in the gold mining business.

Before they experience success, people are sure to meet with temporary defeat and perhaps some failure. When defeat overtakes you, the easiest and most logical thing to do is quit. That is exactly what most people do. Many of the most successful people in this country have said their greatest success came just one step beyond the point at which defeat had overtaken them. Failure is a trickster with a keen sense of irony and cunning. It takes great delight in tripping one when success is almost within reach. It is imperative in the sales profession to continue to strive. Never quit. You have to have a never-ending desire to succeed. It's that strong desire that makes one great.

A good example of someone who has desire is my brother "Dapper" Dan. He's not a salesperson, but he has all the qualities it takes to be great. The qualities discussed in this chapter are required to be successful in everyday life, not just in the sales business. Dan supervises a pipeline company. He sets daily goals so he can do the best job possible. If his men don't meet these goals, who do you think is the first to jump in and help? He not only does this in his business but in his personal life as well. He is the most highly motivated individual I know, and the word *quit* is not in his vocabulary.

There are typical salespeople, and there are great salespeople. The difference between these two is that great salespeople have the desire to become true closers. The difference between earning a great income and a mediocre living is determined by one thing—closing the sale. When you learn the art of closing, you will understand why *only closers make big money*.

2

SALESPEOPLE

Typical salespeople have basic knowledge of the sales process and are generally knowledgeable about the product, but instead of closing, they explain everything from a logical standpoint, without including the emotional triggers required to make the sale. They get so involved in their presentation that they don't know when to shut up. They talk and keep on talking, never closing, and not knowing they have talked past the close. Why bring up more things for the clients to think about when they are ready to buy the product now? You do not have to give all the information all the time. When the customers are ready to buy, close. Everybody loses if you do not—most of all, your client, who will benefit from owning your product. I say "will benefit" from owning your product because I'm assuming you are selling a good product, a product you believe in wholeheartedly.

Typical salespeople take shortcuts by hurrying through their presentation. In addition, typical salespeople fail to ask enough questions to close the sale. This type of salesperson fears their product is

ONLY CLOSERS make BIG MONEY

11

flawed and wants to avoid any mention of these faults instead of confronting them head on.

The typical salesperson doesn't realize that enthusiasm is what motivates people to buy. Because of their negativity, these salespeople think the new top-gun salesperson who is filled with enthusiasm is just lucky. They do not realize that the salesperson's enthusiasm is what makes people want to buy from him or her. They probably had that same enthusiasm at one time, but it is now lost in a muck of negativity.

Enthusiasm is a key ingredient in sales. It is what makes people get emotionally involved in the presentation. Getting people emotionally involved puts them in a decision-making mode. You probably have heard "That guy is so lucky; he gets all the good clients." Ha! I have one thing to say to that: there are no bad clients; there are just bad salespeople. The only thing that makes one client better than another is a great salesperson.

A good friend of mine has a great solution for this type of thinking. He markets a product at seminars and uses this technique in sales training. At some meetings as the people enter the room, they are randomly assigned to a representative. At other times, my friend lets the salespeople pick their own clients, and he takes whoever is left. Guess what happens—he consistently outsells every one of his representatives. Why? Because he is a pro, a closer with a positive attitude.

Great salespeople understand that enthusiasm is contagious and builds the prospect's excitement about the product. Enthusiasm is conveyed in many ways. Gesturing with your hands helps build enthusiasm, and speaking with enthusiasm also helps. You can raise and lower your voice to convey enthusiasm. When you think your prospect is losing interest in your presentation, speak louder to bring his or her attention back to what you are saying.

Great salespeople involve their clients in the presentation. When demonstrating a product, let your customers operate or use the product. Getting them emotionally involved creates excitement within them. By operating the product, the client can see and feel how it can benefit them. For example, if you're selling computers, let the client operate the computer. This helps them sell themselves, which definitely makes your life easier.

Great salespeople know people buy based on their emotions and defend the purchase with logic. They also know how to help the client defend the purchase with logic. For example, while going through the paperwork, a great salesperson says things like, "I am glad to see people so excited about doing nice things like this for themselves and their families. I can see this is a happy event for all of you. More importantly, you work hard for your money, and you deserve it, don't you?" By helping the client defend the purchase with logic, the great salesperson decreases the chances of a cancellation.

Making a sale is great, but a cancellation can definitely put a damper on the day. When a cancellation occurs, the great salesperson understands that they have to take the good with the bad. They put the cancellation out of their mind, knowing negative thoughts can only hinder them.

Great salespeople expect to make a sale at all times. They go into every presentation with this positive attitude. They avoid negative people, knowing these people cannot contribute to their growth. Great salespeople greet people with a warm smile—not just customers in a sales situation but everyone they come into contact with. They understand everyone is a potential customer, and they treat everyone the same.

Great salespeople know they have to make a friend before they can make a sale. They realize the customers have to trust them before they will make a decision to spend their money with the salesperson. They are aware of one basic fact: people must believe in them. Without believing in them, trust cannot be established. Great salespeople never put themselves above clients and never talk down to them. They treat people with the utmost respect and know how to empathize with their clients. They build people up by making them feel good about themselves. Great salespeople know how and when to do this in order to break down sales resistance. If that sales resistance is not broken down, a sale will never be made.

Great salespeople know how to adjust to any situation that comes up. They are like actors on stage and know giving an academy award performance is an important link in making the sale. They adjust their performance to meet any type of personality the customer might have. Their presentation is canned, but it is not given in the same way to every prospect. Their presentation is designed to cover any and all objections and questions, whether hidden or voiced, and can be adjusted at the drop of a hat. They know a hidden objection is the cause of comments such as "I want to think about it," "I never make an instant decision," "I've been ripped off before," "I can't afford it," "I have to talk to someone," or "I'm just looking." Knowing this is the case, they get these hidden concerns to the surface so they can close the sale. Voiced objections are easy to answer and are gladly welcomed. We'll discuss ways that you can get clients to reveal hidden objections in Chapter 8. Unvoiced or hidden objections will kill a sale quicker than anything else.

Great salespeople understand the importance of control. These salespeople control the flow of information. They know that not supplying enough information will prevent a sale. You have to provide enough information about the product—how it will benefit the client, details about the warranty, etc.—in order for the client to want to buy it. But too much information will also hinder a sale. Having to consider more than two or three issues often confuses a client and will prevent him or her from reaching a decision. (We'll discuss controlling the flow of information and other ways to give an effective presentation in Chapter 4.) A great salesperson knows not to give too much or too little information.

You'll know you've provided enough information when the client starts asking questions about the product. That's when you start asking closing questions, such as "You've obviously done your homework. You know that this is the type of automobile you'd like to own, right?" A great salesperson never talks past the close and knows to stop talking after asking a closing question. (Closing is covered in detail in Part 3 of this book.)

Controlling the client's attention is one of the key factors in any sales presentation. One way to gain control is to give your presentation while sitting at the kitchen table during in-home demonstrations. Avoid the den or family room, where the client's attention can wander. When you're seated opposite the client at the table, it's much easier to gain and keep control of his or her attention. When riding in a vehicle, put the wife in the front seat. In most families, the wife is the one who makes the financial decisions. With her in the front seat, you can direct the closing questions to her. (Closing questions are covered in Part 3 of this book.) Paying attention to these little things adds up to making a sale.

Be careful not to be overbearing, but take the client in the direction needed to complete the sale. Great salespeople ask questions and listen to determine who the decision maker is when dealing with a husband and wife. Once this is determined, they direct the closing questions to this person. In most cases, as stated earlier, the wife is the decision maker. Men generally follow their spouse. If the wife does not want the product, the husband usually won't want to displease her. On the other hand, if she wants it, he will want to satisfy her. Great salespeople also know how to work the kids into the presentation. They direct questions to the kids so they help sell the parents. For example, if you're selling resort property, you can show the kids the pool and the tennis courts, and let the children's enthusiasm influence the parents. Paying attention to the children and incorporating them into the presentation makes them the salesperson's advocate.

Great salespeople—closers, in other words—know how to apply subtle and not-so-subtle pressure. They apply subtle pressure by pulling at the client's heart strings. A good way to do this is to tell third-party stories. You could tell a story about another family that you worked with in the past, and about why and how they got involved with the product. (Third-party stories are covered in detail in Chapter 3.) You can apply not-so-subtle pressure through the careful use of intimidation: making direct eye contact and pointing at the client. The best compliment a salesperson can receive is when a client thanks him or her for not applying pressure, and the salesperson knows he had the pressure on throughout the entire presentation.

Closers love the word "no" for two reasons. First, they realize the more NOs they hear, the closer they are to a YES and making a sale. Second, they know how and when to say "no." Saying "no" can be your strongest closing tool. Saying "no" is like taking candy from a baby. The more you take it away by saying "no," the more the clients want your product. For example, when a woman finds a dress she wants to buy, but it's not available in her size, her desire for the dress increases. The simple fact that it's unavailable (which is a way of saying "no") makes her want the dress more. (This closing technique is covered in Chapter 13.)

A closer never judges, but he always qualifies. You can build rapport with a client while qualifying them, by asking questions about their work, the length of time on the job, and their kids and the kids' ages. Ask the wife about her work by asking "do you work outside the home, or are you like my wife who works harder raising our three kids than I do?" This kind of question builds rapport and tells the closer if a second income is available. It's important not to overqualify your client and try to sell them something they can't afford.

For example, if you let a prospect test-drive a new Ford LTD Crown Victoria, but he or she can only afford a pre-owned LTD Crown Victoria that's two years old, you have a problem that could cost you a sale. After qualifying clients properly, the pros sell the customers what they (the pros) decide they need. By doing so, the pro is doing the client a favor because, to use our current example, the client is looking for a car because he needs one. If you fail to qualify the client, his disappointment over not being able to buy the new car may cost you the sale. If you do not qualify your customers and sell them your product, they are probably going to head down the road to a closer that can help them.

Always greet your prospects in the same manner. If you judge someone based on their clothes or the car they drive, thinking they can't afford your product, you've just made a big mistake. You can never determine someone's financial position by material items. Your greeting or the first impression you present should be the same with everyone. If you are not enthusiastic in your greeting because you're judging someone, he or she will feel it, and a sale could be lost before you even get started.

When reviewing presentations, closers look at what went right and what went wrong. Some people believe that you shouldn't review what went wrong, but you can't benefit from your mistakes if you don't analyze them. Never dwell on the negative, but try to analyze what happened so you can improve on it. Reviewing what went right provides positive reinforcement. By looking at both, your sales will improve.

The top producers in the office—the closing machines—are achievers who always strive to win. They help other salespeople in the office by sharing ideas that can make them successful. They don't think that sharing their ideas could help someone outsell them. They believe what goes around comes around and that helping others will benefit them in time. They want everyone working around them to be the best they can be and feel an obligation to help everyone. They don't fear competition. They help others close sales without asking for part of the commission. They have the utmost respect for management and support their decisions when discussing them with others in the office. If they do not have what the client is looking for, they will go out of their way to help the client find it through another source. By doing so, they increase the chance that the customer will return when he or she needs their product. People remember when they're treated with respect and courtesy. When my wife managed a music store, she would call other stores to help her customers if she could not fulfill their needs, and they always remembered this and came back to her many times.

Closers do not get too emotionally high or low; they maintain equanimity. By doing so they remain consistent. When a slight sales slump arises, they are the first to realize it and respond with urgency to counteract it immediately. They are not afraid to approach the hottest salesperson at the time and accompany him or her on a few sales calls. Going on a few sales calls with a hot salesperson can help the presentation of someone who's experiencing a slump. Closers never dwell on the past, always strive forward, and never give up. They love a challenge and are always the ones on the phone making calls for new prospects. They set their goals, always trying to improve their current situation. Once the goals are reached, top producers set new ones, knowing these goals keep advancing them.

When a closer agrees to do something, he or she always follows through, no matter what it takes or costs. If this agreement is with a customer, the closer keeps the agreement, even if it costs their commission. They never waver or back out of a commitment. They never put a commission before the customers' needs and never sell a product they do not believe in. Without believing in a product, they cannot sell it to the best of their ability. If you are selling something you don't really believe in, you won't be able to push your client with pressure, if necessary, or yourself mentally. You should find another product you do believe in, and you will make more money. Closing machines have such confidence in their ability they will spend their own money on mailouts to increase productivity. They know that sometimes you need to spend money to make money.

As an example of a great salesperson, I'd like to tell a story about a true professional I know who runs the sales and marketing for a large condominium developer. I called him recently to see how he was doing. He told me sales were going great, and they were way ahead of their projections for the year. He said they had run into a snag with one lender who had financed over thirty condos. He was personally calling everyone and explaining the situation and holding in the sales. Even though he was on the verge of losing $3 million in sales, he just laughed and said, "Thank goodness everyone can't handle these problems or we wouldn't make the kind of money we do selling. What a great way to make a living."

PART 2: THE PRESENTATION

The mind is like a parachute: if it isn't open, it won't work.
By keeping an open mind and paying attention,
you can learn something every day.
                                    —Mark J. McDonnell

3

TOOL$ OF THE TRADE

The warm-up is a tool you use to overcome the customer's negative feelings toward salespeople. Most people neither like nor trust us. People fear they will be taken unfair advantage of. They think we are going to pressure them into making an unsound decision. Your goal is to remove this fear. Until you do, you can't make a sale.

Most people have an ingrained fear of going to the dentist. When the dentist talks to the patients and asks about their jobs, families, and interests, the patients start to relax. You cannot make a sale until you make a friend. If people do not like you, they won't trust you, and they won't do business with you. Customers should feel you will always be there to service their needs. They have to feel you are not some fly-by-night, here-today-gone-tomorrow salesperson. If they do not buy you, they never will buy your product. So another purpose of the warmup is to make people like you.

A third purpose is to make your prospects feel comfortable. During the warmup, you talk about the prospect's family, jobs, and hobbies. Ask how long they have been employed in their present job. Let them tell you about different aspects of their jobs. Make people feel important about what they do for a living. In addition, talk about their kids and their hobbies such as sports or music. Most people are proud of their children and their children's accomplishments. Relate these achievements to ones made by your own children. Relate their hobbies to your interests and hobbies or to those of your friends. You can tell stories to make your prospects feel comfortable. Put yourself on their level to make them feel comfortable.

Do not start your presentation until the customers are warmed up. You have to develop a gut feeling to determine when they're sufficiently warmed up. When customers start asking you about your family is one indication they're warm. You'll know they're warm when you feel a bond has been established between you and your customers. Some customers require a longer warmup than others. A successful warmup makes the customers receptive to you and your product. Most important, a successful warmup establishes a feeling of trust; the customer trusts you and believes what you say.

You can also qualify customers during the warmup. The purpose of qualifying is to find the money, which you do by asking questions about the client's job—what kind of job it is and how long they've held it. You also want to determine if a second income is available. A second goal of qualifying is to determine what product is right for your client. Qualifying is a closer's most important tool. You have to know the answers to basic questions before you can sell the client. If you don't, you can easily go off on a wild tangent, without knowing what product is right for your client.

Suppose you are selling carpet. You need to know the answers to the following questions:

Have you been looking for carpet very long?

Where have you looked?

Which brand have you liked or disliked? Why?

Which colors have you decided are the best for your home?

Do you have a certain price range per square yard you are looking to stay in?

Which rooms are you going to carpet?

Now let's look at why the answers to these questions are important.

The answer to the first question, "Have you been looking for carpet very long?" tells you how long the customers have been shopping. It also tells you if they are price shopping. If the customer has been shopping for a while and hasn't made a decision, he or she is price shopping (meaning, they'll make their choice based on the lowest price). The more places they've looked, the more salespeople they've encountered who can't close the sale.

Sometimes customers are hesitant to answer the second question, "Where have you looked?" Or they might answer, "oh, a few places" or "this is the first place I have looked." A red flag goes up if they have been looking at other places. You need to know the competition's prices for the same or similar products. Getting this information is part of the homework. You must know your competition. By knowing the competition's prices, you might be able to come down a little on your price and still make a profit for yourself and your company. If yours is the first place the customer has stopped, you must build credibility in your company. You must emphasize the warranties associated with the product and the prompt time in which the carpet can be installed.

The third question, "Which brands have you liked or disliked?" tells you what items, if any, you can eliminate from the discussion. If you have the brand the customer likes, you can show them this brand and close on price, if necessary. Knowing the answer to this question also gives you the opportunity to show another brand of the same quality for less money. If the customer likes it as much as the other brand, you've made a good impression. Trust is built because of your intent to save the customer's money.

Suppose you're showing the customer a particular brand. You can proceed like this:
Have you seen this brand before? How much was it a yard? Is there any reason you didn't buy it? You want to save money, right? Would this price fit in your budget?

The answer to the fourth question, "Which colors have you decided are best for your home?" helps eliminate unnecessary time showing colors not important in making the sale.

The answer to the fifth question, "Do you have a certain price range per square yard you are looking to stay in?" is particularly important because it will tell you the quality of the carpet you're going to sell them. You also need to determine if the prospects are building a new home or if they're recarpeting their existing home. When customers are building a new home, the builder usually gives them a budget for carpeting. If this is the case, ask them to tell you what their budget is. If customers are recarpeting their existing home, ask them how many rooms they're carpeting. Then you can quickly calculate how big the order will be and give them better prices on volume.

The kinds of qualifying questions you ask depend on your product. You have to ask questions that are appropriate to the product you're selling. Properly qualifying a client saves time, and time, in the sales profession, is money.

Now let us look at common mistakes salespeople make when qualifying. One of the biggest mistakes made is to prejudge a client before you ask any questions and then decide they can't afford your product. Most prejudging occurs when a salesperson makes a judgment about a person's buying power based on the clothes they're wearing, the car they drive, the house they own, or how well-groomed they are. These visual cues can provide some information, but you must look beyond these superficialities, keeping an open mind and asking qualifying questions.

When I bought my wife's Lincoln Town car, I told her I was going to test the attitude of the automobile salespeople. I dressed in dirty pants, a stained tee shirt that I wear to work in the yard, and sloppy tennis shoes without socks. While walking around looking at different automobiles on a car lot, I looked up at the showroom, waiting and silently begging for someone to help me. After giving it as much time as I thought was necessary, I left without getting one bit of help. Did some of those salespeople prejudge me by my appearance? Probably! No one came out to assist me. No one came to ask me any qualifying questions. They probably decided by looking at my clothes that I couldn't afford one of their Lincolns. Never prejudge!

A good friend of mine once told me a similar story. He sold real estate for a land development company. A couple drove up in a beat up old car. The husband hadn't shaved in a couple days and was dressed in old Levis and tennis shoes with holes in them. They came in and proceeded to buy a piece of property. The husband walked out to his car and came back with a paper sack full of one hundred dollar bills and paid cash. If my friend had prejudged them, he never would have made the sale.

I can provide many stories similar to these. The bottom line is to never prejudge, always qualify.

The true professional qualifies a prospect during the warmup, determining what product they can afford. Remember the example provided in Chapter 2 about test-driving a new Crown Victoria when a prospect can only afford a preowned one? A common problem you'll encounter is that everybody wants something bigger, better, more comfortable, faster, and more efficient. The problem is that bigger, better, more comfortable, faster, and more efficient usually means more money. In most cases, a sales line offers different products at various prices. Why blow a sale when our client can afford x and not y? X could be a used Crown Victoria, a year old, not a new one. X could be a boat with 5.0 liter engine, not a 5.7 liter. X could be a two-bedroom condominium, not a three-bedroom. X could be a lakeview lot, not a lakefront lot. X could be a mid-demand week, not a high-demand week, in a timeshare. Before going into an all-out sales presentation, you must decide which product in your sales line the customer can afford.

A good friend of mine is a consultant for time-share developers. He was employed to review all sales and marketing for a developer in Colorado. This particular company did in-home presentations prior to inviting potential customers to their resorts. They wanted to qualify these prospects before inviting them for a complimentary three-day, two-night stay. This, obviously, can be very expensive if the prospects who come cannot afford or have no interest in the product. My friend observed that all the representatives went into a high-powered presentation on all the benefits of owning high-demand time. After going out on sales calls with different representatives during the week, he went to the resorts the following weekend to review the sales program. He was not surprised to see that when a sale took place it was always a high-demand week or nothing at all. Why? The prospects were only interested in high-demand because all they were told about in the home were the benefits of high-demand. The developer had one high-demand season in his inventory for every ten mid- or low-season weeks.

In order to resolve this problem, my friend revamped the in-home presentation to give the benefits of the overall program. The reps were trained not to pinpoint a certain type of product as high, mid, or low. In the following months, all different types of the product were being sold at the resorts. Previously, many people could not afford the high season and wanted to wait until they could. Then they ended up never owning anything. After the program was revamped, people were buying the product they could afford. Sales not only increased, but inventory, earlier not sold, was being sold at a regular pace. The developer and salespeople were happy, but more importantly their customers were satisfied.

Qualifying, not prejudging, is one of the most important professional skills you can develop. You should include it in every warmup and do it gracefully. True closers know this. That's why they make as much money as they do and will continue to make it throughout their careers.

Another important tool is third-party stories. Stories sell! People do not want to be told what to do, but if you relate their situation to someone else's situation, they don't feel pressured or threatened. It's reassuring to know that someone else has been in the same situation. When they hear about someone in a similar situation, they offer a decision similar to the one the other client made. For example, suppose a client said something like "I don't know if I'm ready to start investing in real estate." Your response should be something like this:
You remind me of a client I worked with a month ago. He felt the same way. He was afraid of investing, but after weighing all the benefits, he decided, why not? He could keep his money in the bank where it was paying him very little after taxes, or invest in real estate. He chose to invest because it just makes good common sense. Don't you agree?

Here's another example. Suppose a client said "I really like this piano but it sure is a lot of money." Your reply would be something like this:

> You remind me of a gentleman I helped the other day. He mentioned that he'd been looking at pianos on and off for several years. Every time he looked at the high quality pianos that he wanted to own, the price had gone up. He decided that if he didn't invest in one now, chances are he'd never be able to afford one. Whether you can afford one next year or not isn't really important. What is important is saving the money you can by taking advantage of the opportunity now. Don't you agree?

Third party stories help people make decisions without having to pressure them. Sometimes people don't want to make a decision, but knowing somebody else has makes them feel more comfortable. In addition, stories keep your clients interested. Your prospects will be more attentive if you tell a story related to their situation. A story that relates another's experience to their situation will get a client's attention quicker than anything else. Suppose a client asks you "What type of warranty comes with the hot tub?" You could respond with "Two years with parts and labor included." But all you are doing here is giving a dry answer. You need to use all your ammunition such as in the following response:

> You know, it's funny you asked. A gentleman and his wife invested in this same model yesterday. You see we have such confidence in our engineers and manufacturing that we have a two-year warranty that includes parts and labor. He told us that was the best warranty he's found on the market. He and his wife had been looking at different hot tubs, and he told me we must have a lot of confidence in our product to offer such a warranty. We believe by building them

right in the first place a lot of money is saved in need-less and wasted service calls. Makes sense. Doesn't it?

As you can see in this example, you can use a third-party story not only to explain the warranty but also to cover other important points. First, someone who got involved in your product asked the same question. Second, you let your current customer know someone else had already done some shopping around. Third, you build value in the product by telling the customer you build the product right in the first place. This justifies your price.

When telling stories, make sure they are true. If you look back at different sales you have made, you can always remember situations that could be used to sell your product to the next customer. If you are new in the sales profession, get your manager or other sales-people to tell you situations you can use as a third-party story. You can always tell your prospect what happened with one of your associates or your manager.

Many years ago I was thinking about taking on a new challenge. I knew I could do sales training. One day I was wandering around the mall while my wife shopped. I stopped at a piano store. My wife wanted a piano so our son could take lessons. She informed me that kids who are musically inclined were more well adjusted, earned better grades in school, and tended to be more disciplined. In the piano store, I started talking to the manager. He showed me a few different pianos, and I said, "Isn't it amazing how music will help kids make better grades in school and become more well adjusted later in their lives?" He asked, "Where did you hear that?" I said, "I'm not sure but it sure sounds good." He laughed and asked me what I did for a living. I told him I was in sales and sales training. We agreed I could help his sales people. We ended up trading my sales training for partial payment of a piano.

In many cases, people don't buy the product, they buy the story. But in any case, stories sell, and you will too if you use them.

4

ELEMENTS OF AN EFFECTIVE PRESENTATION

This chapter covers the presentation and the qualities of a good one. First and foremost, a presentation should be simple. An effective presentation builds credibility in you and your organization, value in your product, and enthusiasm in your prospects. Your presentation should never downgrade the competition. Later in this chapter, I provide effective ways for you to deal with the competition without downgrading it. Finally, when giving a presentation, you should listen to and observe your prospects. Their words and body language will give you important clues as to how effective your presentation is and how the prospects are responding to you.

KEEP IT SIMPLE, STUPID–KISS

A saying used in a profession or an organization can come to represent that organization. The saying in the Marine Corps is *semper fi*, always faithful. In sports it's *when the going gets tough, the tough get going.* In the sales profession, *keep it simple stupid* is a saying that should be understood completely. How can someone make a decision if he or she is confused? Most people get confused if more than two or three issues are involved. The more choices available, the greater the chance your prospect will get confused. You aren't going to sell a car to someone who test drives every model on the lot. You aren't **ONLY** going to sell a copying machine if you demonstrate every model.

A friend of mine was marketing a subdivision. Part of the marketing strategy was a presentation and tour of the property, which normally lasted about three hours. One of his salesmen went on tour at 9:00 in the morning and was not back at 5:00 that evening. Believing that a serious mishap had occurred, my friend was ready to call the police. About 6:00 the salesman came in, looking as if he had been dragged through the trenches. My friend asked him what in the world had happened. The salesman had shown every lot on the inventory–over two hundred! And the clients did not buy even one of the two hundred lots they saw. How could they make a decision when they were in a confused state of mind?

Some products have so many good qualities, salespeople often oversell them. True, value will always justify the price, but too much value can be too good to be true. A friend of mine sells a product with so many options that to explain all of them would confuse almost anybody. He points out only the highlights of the product depending on what his prospect is looking for. If he explained all the options, he would never make a sale. When the prospects discover the extra options, they feel they have bought something that was better than they thought. By describing only two or three options, he simplifies his presentation and avoids making his product sound too good to be true.

While I was attending a boat show in St. Louis, I encountered a truly great salesperson exhibiting a housewares package. He completely mesmerized me and the entire crowd. The machine he was demonstrating was amazing. It had many different qualities. In spite of all it could do, he only demonstrated two or three things the machine could do. If he had shown all it could do, he would have sacrificed the full effect of his demonstration. He made his presentation simple and to the point while keeping the crowd's complete attention. After he made the sales (which were quite a few), he gave everyone a brochure showing additional qualities of the product. This information was a bonus for the people who had bought the product. I was quite impressed.

BUILDING CREDIBILITY

Your presentation should establish the credibility of your company. People want to know that you are going to be around to service their accounts and take care of any problems that might arise in the future. They want to know how financially solid the company is so they feel comfortable doing business with you. People often buy products because of the name attached to them and because they feel comfortable doing business with that company. Credibility is often lost in the sales process but is necessary in all sales presentations. Many sales people only talk about their product and fail to build credibility in the company they represent. Salespeople often give dynamic presentations and think they've definitely made a sale, but then discover that they've lost it. When you find you've lost a sale and don't know why, in most cases it's because you failed to build credibility in your company.

Think about different commercials you see on television or ads you see in newspapers. Most companies that have been in business for a period of years include that in the advertising: "serving your needs for over 30 years," "since 1923," or "family-owned for generations." These statements build credibility. "We have been here and we will always be here to service your needs if any problems arise" is often the most powerful selling point that can be made.

When you build credibility, you'll be surprised to hear customers ask, "If you were in our shoes, what type of financing would you choose?" Or "If you were in our shoes, would you pay cash or finance?" These questions are the easy ones to answer. And customers ask them because they believe in you and your company.

BUILDING VALUE

Value justifies a purchase. It can overcome the cost of any product. If the customer believes the product has value, the dollar amount is generally not important (as long as it is not totally out of line). Salespeople get it into their heads that the reason certain competitors sell more is that their price is lower. Hogwash! Great salespeople know that selling short on value will kill you every time. They realize that building the company's credibility, informing the client of the warranties and services they offer, and emphasizing that the company will always be there to help its clients outweighs the price of the product. Clients won't balk at the price if all these bases are covered.

Here's what happened to me when I was out shopping for a new boat one day. I had been looking at different brands and models for some time. I knew the size and basic features I was looking for, and most were competitively priced. I saw one boat that was absolutely beautiful, with the features I was looking for, but I was quoted a price about $5,000 more than others with the same features. I was curious to know why this brand was so much more costly. And that's when I met a great salesperson.

He proceeded to show how this boat was constructed differently. He explained the differences in the grade of upholstery his company insisted on using. He explained that because better quality materials were used in this boat, his company could offer a better warranty than other companies could. In the course of our conversation he found out what type of boat I owned and how long I had owned it. He introduced me to the service manager and showed me the service department. All of this built confidence in his company and the value of the boat. After he assured me that the company would be there if I ever needed any assistance, he took me back to the showroom so I could drool some more. Finally, he looked me in the eye and said, "You see, Dave, if I'd met you eight years ago you wouldn't be looking for a new boat today." I looked up rather curious; "why?" I asked. He looked me straight in the eye again and said, "If you had bought one of these eight years ago when you bought your present boat, you wouldn't need a new one today. This will be the last boat you will ever own. You won't need another one because this one will last you the rest of your life." I was done—well done.

Building value is the key to closing. Great salespeople spend most of their time setting up the close by doing the things outlined in this chapter. When we play billiards the key to winning is setting up your next shot. By playing position we have the chance to run the table on our opponent. We have to be in line at all times during the demonstration to make the sale. The closing then takes very little time.

Sometimes prospects will say that they can buy a comparable product for less money. Well, that's fine, but is the warranty as extensive? Is the pump on the hot tub a two horse power instead of a one and a half horse power? Does the other company offer free service calls for an extended period of time? Is the slate on the pool table three-quarters of an inch thick? Is the cash value on the policy the same? Does the advertising penetrate the same market? I could go on and on. Write down the qualities of your product, and use your list to build value. If your client believes your product is valuable, the price will not be a big issue. People need to know that a lower price is insignificant if the product won't last. I think most people would have the same response that I had if they were presented with a sale the way my boat was presented to me. If you do not get this point across, everyone loses. Your clients lose because they are going to be disappointed in the future with a product that has to be replaced, and you have lost a sale that could have made you and your customers prosper. The prospects have to feel the product is worth their investment. They have to understand how the product will benefit them before they give you their hard-earned money. They have to see excellence in the merchandise so they can take advantage of the opportunity. Prospects need to know the quality of the goods in order to be motivated to buy.

NEVER DOWNGRADE THE COMPETITION

I've seen this happen too many times. Prospects mention the competitor's product, and the salesperson says, "Oh! you'd never want to buy from them. They never service their owners. Their product is sub-par. I've heard horror stories from people who bought that product." This drives the customer away—away from you and your product. When you downgrade the competition, you are implicitly telling your customers to shop around, because hearing you bad-mouth the competition makes people feel that you are afraid of their finding a better product.

Agree with them when they praise the competition, say something like "they have a good product," "they do a good job," or "they have fine engineers behind their product." By saying this, you are implying that you are not afraid of another product. They are thinking "at last a salesperson who is honest and straight with me. I like this person. He's not trying to cram his product down my throat."

Some people feel if you don't bad-mouth the competition, the prospects will go looking somewhere else. They won't if you follow up with all the benefits of your product. Make the prospects feel comfortable with you and your product. Describe the qualities of your product that separate it from all the rest. You don't need to mention the product they brought up, but compare your product to most of the other products similar to yours. By doing this, your prospect won't ONLY feel you are attacking a particular product or trying to defend yours. You are showing why your particular product stands out in the marketplace. People generally don't want to waste time shopping around if they can find a product that's valuable.

By pointing out the positive values of your product, you can eliminate your competition without downgrading them. For example, you can say "most companies give a one-year warranty on their products. We give a two-year warranty because we want you as customers for years to come. We also want you telling your friends about us. You see, you are our best advertising source, and we want to make sure you are completely satisfied." What you've done is eliminate any competition that gives less warranty than your company does. Or you can compare the qualities of the product: "most pumps are one and a half horse power. We put two horse power pumps on our hot tubs for durability and to move more water." Again, you eliminate the competition by pointing out another advantage of owning your product.

When you know what the competition has to offer, you can emphasize the benefits of your product. Write down the benefits, and then determine what the benefits of your competitors' products are. You can always find something in any product that has benefits over others. The key is to learn the competition's product inside out. Always build on the finer points of your product.

If you say, "*No* other company has this or that," and your prospects then learn that one company does, you are out of a sale. The clients automatically lose trust in you. By saying *most* companies don't have this or that, you won't encounter this problem. If a prospect says, "Well, ABC Company has that feature." You can reply, "Yes, they are one of the few that do." Then you can go into the overall benefits of your company and product and close the sale. If they bring up that XYZ Company also has a two horsepower pump in their hot tub, answer with, "Yes, they are one of the few that does. What else about their product do you like?" They then will tell you how to sell them. They are history! It's over! Listen and agree that your competitor's product is very good. Then compare the superior benefits of your product and close. Downgrading the competition is just not necessary, and you should never ever do it.

TAKING CONTROL

As we discussed in Chapter 2, you need to take control in order to direct the prospect towards the close. In that chapter I stated that great salespeople need to qualify their clients and sell them what they decide the prospects need. There are two general views on this matter: 1) the salesperson decides what the client needs and sells it to the client, and 2) always sell the clients what they want.

Both views are right to a certain degree. Listening to the prospect tells you which of these approaches to use. If the prospect wants item Z and he can afford item Z, then sell him item Z. But a problem arises if he cannot afford item Z. Previously I told a story about test-driving a Crown Victoria when the prospect could afford only a pre-owned, two-year-old one. In actuality people come in to a dealership and want a new car. Let us say they are driving a ten-year-old car that is run down and is costing them money with repairs. I know that driving a two-year-old car is going to save them money on unnecessary maintenance. If they want the new Crown Victoria and cannot afford it, they end up buying nothing. Then who loses? Sure I lose a sale, but these people are back to the old car that is costing them money everyday. These people are the real losers because I did not solve their problem. If I can get them into a car that solves their problem, it is a win/win situation. I have made a sale, and they are happy owning an almost new car. By controlling the clients and directing them to what they can afford, everyone wins.

Another form of control is knowing when listening gets out of control. Sometimes people start talking, which is your goal, but you can't get a word in edgewise. You have to take control of the conversation or you will never be able to give your presentation. I caution you to be careful here. If you cut them off too soon, you might miss some important information. Making this judgment call is really a double-edged sword. Just remember, do not be too quick to take over, but do not let the prospects control the conversation. Take control and lead them. Do not let them lead you or you are sunk. It is important to have this control from start to finish.

A presentation is like walking down a hallway with doors on each side. We might have to veer to the left, then back to the right, but we have to get to the end. We have to close the doors along the way as we get to them. We have to be focused on the final outcome. We listen and adjust, but we have to keep on going, directing and controlling as we go.

We have to guide our clients in the direction *we* want them to go. We have to govern their thoughts by instructing them.

By legislating the flow of the presentation or demonstration, we sway them in our direction.

BUILDING ENTHUSIASM

Enthusiasm produces sales by getting people to be emotional. Remember, emotion is what pushes people to decision making. If your speech is in the same tone all the time, you will put your client to sleep. Intonation has to be implemented in all presentations. By this I mean raising and lowering the pitch and volume of your voice at certain key spots to keep people's attention. Observe your clients while you talk, and if you see their attention wandering, raise your voice. Another effective way to create excitement is using body language. This keeps people up mentally. Public speakers are real pros at this art. They speak to hundreds of people at one time. In any large group, minds have a tendency to wander. The speakers use their hands, their arms, and they walk across the front of the room to keep people focused on them. You can point directly at your client to get their complete attention. You can make "follow me" gestures to invite their agreement. You can also make a halt motion with the palm of your hand to use with downselling, implying, "stop, this is what you need." (The art of downselling is explained in Chapter 5.) Enthusiasm lights a fire under the dead. If you have enough enthusiasm, you can motivate anybody. It will create interest in your product. It builds desire and will capture your clients' attention. Your enthusiasm will make your customers enthusiastic. When they are enthusiastic, they will make decisions with emotion.

Your customers have to be stimulated to make a decision. Their minds have to be captivated before they will agree to buy your product. You have to inspire them enough to get them involved. They have to be satisfied within themselves in order to make a decision. They have to have eagerness, which makes them come alive.

PLANTING SEEDS

Farmers plant seeds in the fields to grow crops, and once the crops grow, they can cultivate them and take them to market so they can make money. Right? Likewise, in sales, seeds are planted during the presentation not only to cultivate at the close but also to overcome objections, which are very often the same objections you'll encounter over and over. Seeds are statements or questions planted in the subconscious mind to overcome objections and create an atmosphere for the sale.

Depending on the product, four or five objections are usually raised. They come up time and time again. Once you become familiar with these objections, you have to drop seeds to eliminate them before they come up. If you wait until they appear, it might be too late. By waiting until the finish we get caught in a position of having to be defensive. We end up defending ourselves, our product, and the company. By planting seeds, and therefore dismissing the objections during the presentation, we make closing a much easier task.

"I want to think about it" is a commonly encountered objection. Sometimes our prospect does have to think about it. But in most cases this objection is a signal telling us we have to get more information out of our clients to find the real reason for their wanting to think about our offer. When you notice that the same objections are raised over and over, eliminate them up front before the close. If this is not done you will get the old "I want to think about it" response.

Let's say we are showing a commercial building a little far out of town. Drop this seed: "This building is only twenty minutes from downtown. Isn't it amazing how we measure distance by time and not miles in today's world?" The building may be 20 miles away, but it's only 20 minutes away. This seed addresses the client's thought that the building is too far away before they've even vocalized their objection. In another situation, we might be selling lots in a subdivision. Let us say the particular lot our prospect *qualifies* for is on the side of a hill. Our tour would show homes on the side of hills and point out the unique designs, styles, and views of these homes. We do this prior to showing the property we have in mind for this client. If we do it after showing the property, it is too late.

Since we know the basic objections that are going to come up, the law of averages tells us that we have to eliminate them up front, or they will haunt us on the back end. Dismiss them by planting seeds. By planting seeds, known objections can be overcome, and the close can be set up.

Let's use another example. Suppose you're selling boats, and the highest speed of these boats is 45 mph. You can plant this seed, "Most people waterski at only 25 to 35 mph because of the danger involved in going faster." This seed has eliminated the possible objection that the boat isn't fast enough by suggesting that it's too dangerous to go any faster.

Since we know the objections that are going to come up, we need to eliminate them throughout the sales presentation from beginning to end. Responding to objections that the customer verbalizes is covered in detail in Chapter 8.

LISTEN, LISTEN, LISTEN

How in the world can we ever make a sale unless we listen to our clients? Shut up and let the clients tell you how and when to close. Sales is 70 to 80 percent listening and 20 to 30 percent selling. If we listen, we know what seeds to plant and when and where to use trial closes with tie-downs. A trial close with a tie-down is the act of getting an agreement on something relatively minor. If you ask the question in the right way, most of the time the client will answer the way you want. For example, here's a tie-down I often use, "Then this is something you'd like to do, right?" (We'll cover tie-downs in more detail in Chapter 7.)

Sometimes we are so caught up in wanting to talk we do not let people tell us how to sell them. Suppose a client asks if the product is available in the color red. The salesperson should respond with a simple "yes, we have it in red." But suppose he responds, "yes, we have it in red. We also have it in aqua, fuscia, magenta, mauve, khaki, etc." This salesperson is providing unnecessary information and has probably talked past the close. Listen for the clues to make the sale. Eliminate unimportant information. If we get enough information from a client, we can put them in a position to sell themselves. It would be nice if everyone walked in and said, "I am sold on your product. How much money do you need?" But since that never happens, we must rely on listening because it helps us position ourselves so we can get the ones that might have walked out the door.

Here is a common scenario. How many times have you had a conversation with someone and your mind wanders? You start thinking of something that happened the other day. Your mind just goes to never-neverland. You come back to the conversation, and all of a sudden realize that you have no clue as to what has been said. You have to say, "Could you repeat that?"

This scenario happens in our demonstrations all the time. People are talking, and we start thinking about our last client or some problem at work or home. Important closing information could have been brought up by the prospect, and we have missed it. Shame on us!

Stay focused, and listen so this will not happen to you. Sometimes staying focused is very tough. We have to make a concentrated effort on every presentation not to let our minds wander. It is tough at times but necessary for closing the sale.

We need to listen intently and build people up and compliment them. They do not want to hear about all the things we know or do. Let the clients talk about themselves so you can get into their heads and hearts. The more you let people talk, the more they know you care about their needs and the more information you can process in order to sell them what they need.

Do not get me wrong. At times we have to step in and start selling because some people can just talk forever, and if we do not get a word in, a sale cannot be made. The way to do this without being rude is to take what they say and enter it into your presentation. For example, suppose you're selling resort property, and your client is a proud grandmother who talks continually about her grandkids. You can say, "I'm glad you brought them up! Let me show you what we have for kids." Then you can show her all the features that her grandkids would like. When you see the conversation is getting out of hand, you need to take control.

True pros realize that all information is important; thus, they listen intently to everything that's said. They never close their minds or shut anyone out. They need information like a linebacker needs head-on contact. We can learn from people from all walks of life. Be attentive to every little detail that the client says. Remember to listen, listen, listen, and you'll start closing more sales.

OBSERVING BODY LANGUAGE

By watching the body language of your customers, you'll learn when and where to go with your presentation. When we meet a prospect, a brick wall is usually in the way because people generally do not trust salespeople. Before the sales process begins we have to knock the wall down.

The following are negative signals that you can detect by watching your clients' body language:

Crossing legs with hands on chin

Leaning back in chair with arms crossed

Shaking legs up and down

Not looking directly in your eyes

Not sitting down

Shaking the head sideways

These signals will usually appear after your initial introduction to your customer. Until these signals disappear, do not start closing. As long as the client has assumed one of these postures, you know you need more time to warmup the client and get him to trust you. Until this is accomplished, you should not begin with the core of your presentation. Back up, and go back over something (anything!) or come up with something new. These signals mean you haven't raised the clients' interest level yet.

The following are positive signals to watch for:

Shaking the head up and down

Moving closer to the table

Moving eyebrows up and eyes lighting up

These signs tell you to proceed or begin your close. When the client is signaling you in a positive manner that means the wall is down. The customers are giving you the consent to go ahead. It is time to start trial closing: get minor commitments, and then go for the money!

PRESENTATION BOOKS

Presentation books can be used as sales aids to keep your prospects' attention. When your prospects' minds start to wander, these tools can be used to bring them into the sales scenario. When you know the information in your presentation book like the back of your hand, you have power and are in full control.

Presentation books can also be set up to overcome objections. You explain something to the prospect and then support it with charts, newspaper articles, photographs, etc. Since your presentations have a basic flow, the books need to follow the order of the presentation. Obviously, not all sales presentations are going to be exactly the same or have the same flow. Sometimes we have to interrupt the flow to answer our customers' questions. You must avoid fumbling around trying to find an article that applies to a particular subject of the presentation.

A great salesperson understands that talk alone does not always sell. When a customer can see articles from newspapers, magazines, or photographs concerning the product, the chances for a sale will increase. Editorials and magazine and newspaper articles that relate to your product add credibility to your presentation. But be sure the articles in your book are current. If the material in your presentation book has dates from several years back, you can lose credibility. Always keep your books updated and replace dirty and ratty looking pages. Outdated, dirty, ratty pages cheapen your product. A salesperson who is neatly groomed and who has a neatly presented book goes into a presentation with a much better chance of making the sale. If presentation books are not set up to flow from one point to the next, they can and will confuse your prospects.

It's important to know where your information is at all times, and keep it in order so you know how and when to get to it if necessary. If clients come to see you give your presentation and you also have a tour to show your product, prepare two books: one for the office and one for your car. You never know when you are going to need this backup book. There is nothing worse than being unprepared when *the* moment occurs. Preparation is power, and power makes sales.

5

DOWNSELLING

Downselling is the act of directing customers to the product we have decided they should own. Why would we decide what customers should own and not let them make that decision? It's because they might not be able to afford what they want. When this is the case, we have to decide what they can afford.

As I stated previously, everybody wants something bigger, better, and nicer, but not everybody can afford it. Salespeople have to direct customers to an alternative choice that is better suited for them. Obviously, this choice is one the customer should believe they have made. If we guide the client to the right product, we become a teacher or consultant. The clients value our help because we are giving them beneficial information. Whatever product we decide is right for them to own must be a quality product that will do the job for them.

Prior to starting in the sales profession, I was driving an old beat up car that was not suitable for showing real estate to clients. Before I could start my new career selling real estate, there was one prerequisite:

ONLY CLOSERS 49 make BIG MONEY

I had to buy a new car. All the salespeople I would be working with drove big luxurious cars, and of course, I wanted to drive a big luxurious car.

I was on the car lot looking at gorgeous cars when a salesman approached and introduced himself. That is when I met my first great salesperson. At the time I didn't even know it. He quickly found out that I was just starting in a new profession. If he had let me ooh and aah at the nice new Cadillacs, he could have lost a sale because I could not afford one, and he definitely knew it. I will never forget what he said. "Dave, this is not the car you need now. Six months or a year from now, this car is what you will want, but I have something that would be perfect for you now, and it costs half as much as this." He proceeded to show me a beautiful car that had just been traded in and looked like new. When we took the car for a test drive, he continued, "You see, Dave, there's no sense in having a big payment just starting out in your new job. This car will be more than adequate, and you won't have the pressure on you to make high payments. Now that I've gotten to know you, I know you are going to do great in sales. Once you start getting some big commission checks, I'll take this car in on a new one. Doesn't that make sense?" What could I say to that logic? I had to agree. Now let's look back at exactly what transpired.

I came on the lot and within minutes the salesman prequalified me by asking me about my job. Knowing I was starting out in a new profession, this pro did not want to oversell me on something I could not afford. What if he had let me drive that big beautiful Cadillac? I would have had to walk out, drive to another dealer, and shop around until somebody sold me something. He never even let me in the new Cadillac. He directed me to what he decided I needed and could afford. Did he make me believe it was my decision? Absolutely! Did he advise me and help me like a teacher or consultant would?

Absolutely! Did he come off as a salesperson? Absolutely not! He gave me valuable information and helped me avoid making a mistake by getting in over my head. Did I go back in six months to trade in my car for something bigger, better, and nicer? Absolutely!

The art of downselling is to let the customers believe you will sell them the product they want by directing them to the product that is best for them. They have to believe it is their decision, not yours; and you have to applaud their decision. Give them credit for making a wise choice. If you do this correctly, they will thank you for helping them make such a smart decision. They actually made the decision. They just did not have all the information they needed to come to the final conclusion, and this is where you as a great salesperson step in and supply the needed information. After you do this, the customers can make the final decision, and you can close the sale.

This is another example of how salespeople encounter the objection "I'll think about it." I would have walked out of that car dealership giving a lame excuse to save face. People do not want to tell us they cannot afford the product because their pride won't let them. "I'll think about it" is easier to say and preserves their self-esteem. By downselling from the Cadillac to the other automobile, this great salesperson let me keep my self-respect. I bought a beautiful car, and this great salesperson closed the sale. The decision he chose for me was the right one. I was very happy with my new car, and when I went back to trade it in on another one, he was more than fair. This was a win, win situation. Remember, a good situation should be a good situation for all parties concerned.

6

RESCISSIONS AND MANAGERITIS

Let's talk about a dreaded situation that haunts all salespeople. In today's sales world many products have a cancellation period or cooling off time. State and federal authorities have implemented the rescission period to protect consumers. Personally, I like these laws and think they were long overdue. As professional salespeople, why would we want customers who wanted their money back and couldn't cancel the transaction? That's ridiculous! Why would we want people bad-mouthing the company and/or the product when their dissatisfaction could be resolved by giving these prospects their money back? We would never have a chance to share our product with their referrals. Referrals are absolute gold in the sales business. Besides, they make our job a lot easier because our closing percentage will be a lot higher with referrals. If these people were sold properly from the start, they would not want to cancel in the first place.

ONLY CLOSERS make 53 BIG MONEY

Don't get me wrong–even great salespeople have rescissions. If they don't, they are not getting the close ones. But cancellations can be reduced with certain sales techniques. Before we discuss some of these, I must have your complete attention when I say *never, ever, sell on rescission!* Sales managers, district managers, regional managers, whoever: *never let anybody sell on rescission!* This is the absolute weakest sale ever and will make salespeople weak. Lazy salespeople are the ones who sell like this because it is the path of least resistance.

Don't mistake the point I am making. If a prospect asks if there is a cancellation period, we have to address the issue. Here's one scenario:

"If we go ahead and sign all the papers today, do we have any type of cancellation period?"

"Yes, you do. You have a ten-day grace period, which is stated in the paperwork. However, I don't want you to do anything that you are not completely sure of. I want you completely happy and sure when you leave here today. I'd rather you not get involved than have you call me in a few days telling me you can't go through with the transaction. What exactly do you folks have to consider before going on with this investment?"

Find out what the problem is, and go back to the high points in the presentation that will make a solid sale.

People buy some products strictly on excitement without using any logic, but after the excitement has faded, they have to be able to logically defend their purchase. When selling these types of products (for example, recreational-type products such as boats), remember that people buy as a result of their emotional attachment to the product, but they have to defend their purchase with logic. Someone who goes to a boat show will get excited and put in an order for a boat. When their excitement has faded, they have to be able to defend the purchase. When you see this happening and you don't help them defend the purchase with logic, cancellations will occur. Once they decide to buy your product and the paperwork is done, you need to cement this type of sale. Using the boat example, you can emphasize how the boat will enable the client's family to do something together and how much fun the client's kids will have, and so on. Once all copies are made, put the clients' documents in a manila envelope, sit down, and list all the reasons your clients got involved with you, your product, and your company. Have them help you write the list. Here's an example:

"Mr. and Mrs. Jones, I'm happy to have you as new owners. From the looks on your faces I'm not nearly as happy as you are. Right? Can you do me a small favor? Being with you folks today made me think of something that could be of great assistance to me. So I can express to my future clients the same feeling shown by you today, I'd like to know the reasons you invested in our product."

You should come up with the most important reason first to help get them started. Always list these items on the outside of the manila envelope. After listing several items, excuse yourself to make a copy for yourself. Come back and continue with the following:

"Today we have covered quite a bit of information. Do you have any questions before you go?"

Answer these questions thoroughly; then continue:

"We discussed the cancellation period. I want to be absolutely sure you feel good about this before you leave. If you are not 110 percent sure, I wouldn't feel good about it. You are happy with what you did today. Right?"

If they respond affirmatively, you continue "Great! I just want to be sure all your questions have been answered before you leave."

If you feel they have any apprehensions, stop! Find out what your clients are concerned about. Go back over these concerns, or chances are they will cancel. Many common salespeople want these concerns to disappear without addressing them, which is wishful thinking. The only thing disappearing is the sale. You have to dig in and be strong, or you lose.

Here is another situation that will kill you if not handled properly. When working with both husband and wife, one consents to go ahead with the sale while the other has not been completely sold. Here is how it goes:

"I think it is something we should go ahead with. How about you?" (husband)

"Whatever you think is all right by me." (wife)

Stop! Many salespeople will proceed. They write up the sale only to get a call the next day with a cancellation. Both parties were not sold. Many times the person withholding the consent (in this case, the wife) doesn't want to say anything at that particular moment. Maybe she has an objection that has not surfaced. Reply with, "I'm sure it's okay for him to go ahead, ma'am. But I wouldn't feel good about this unless you feel the same way as he does. How do you really feel?"

This will bring any problem to the surface. If problems are handled in a straightforward manner, there is no reason for most cancellations. Many salespeople don't handle these situations at the point of sale. They hope they can just write up the sale and pray a cancellation will not occur. Wrong! Handle these situations, and cancellations will be reduced.

MANAGERITIS

In many sales organizations the best salespeople don't make the best managers. Some salespeople don't have the patience to understand why other salespeople can't be as good as they are. These salespeople can sell, but they might not be able to convey to other people how to make sales. They lack the knack to train people. In addition, they don't delegate time-consuming duties. They get caught up in details that someone else could do faster and more efficiently, instead of spending time increasing profits for the company. These people are just good at what they do, and that is selling–not managing. These folks should just sell and stay where they will be happiest, making more money for themselves and their company.

However, some organizations are set up so that the best salespeople can and will be good managers if directed properly. These are companies in which managers oversee others and also join in to help close sales. Many products such as cars, land, timeshare, musical instruments, health clubs, boats, etc. are sold in this manner. Salespeople do the selling, but managers do the closing. In this system a dreaded disease will ruin a manager. It is called *manageritis*.

Salespeople get to this level of management because they have proven to be top salespeople. They have been there in the trenches, selling day in and day out. Then they're promoted to manager, and this illness sets in.

Those of you who have this disease know who you are. Let's try to understand how you develop this sickness. As stated, you have proven yourselves. You have established your ability to make sales in your previous role as a salesperson. The big promotion to manager came along, and everything is all right for a while. Then you start getting busy doing things that don't produce sales. You begin making excuses, doing paperwork, sitting behind the desk in your office acting busy. Sometimes you think you are being productive doing these chores. Pretty soon you are closing less and less. As time passes, you lose confidence in your ability to do the thing that used to come so easy. You don't want to go out and look incompetent to your salespeople. You have this fear-of-failure complex.

Take a look at what got you where you are today: it was your ability to close sales. In order to build trust and gain the respect of your salespeople, you must stay in the trenches with them. Get back in there, and all that made you what you are will come back to you. Trust me. Sometimes our egos can keep us down. We want our salespeople to hold us in high regard. Quit being a ghost. Get back in the trenches with them. If you keep hiding, you will never get their respect. You have to earn their allegiance.

A good friend of mine who runs a real estate development company has his managers take out customers every week, sometimes two or three times a week. He never lets them forget where they came from. Staying close to sales keeps them sharp. He doesn't let them hide. When salespeople see their managers doing what the salespeople do with a great deal of success, it builds respect for their managers, and these salespeople will listen to their managers and do what they ask without hesitation. The result is more sales, which means more money for everybody.

A manager can't stay on top and be sharp if he or she is not out on the floor closing sales. A manager who makes sales can more effectively train his salespeople. There is no better high than making a sale. If you're a manager, you can feel good about yourself again. Get out and sell! You deserve it. Don't you?

7

USING TIE-DOWNS

The tie-down is one of the salesperson's most important tools. You use tie-downs to get minor commitments needed in order to make the sale. When you make a statement about the product you're selling, it is essential to follow with a tie-down, such as "don't you agree?" It is necessary to get as many YESes as possible during your presentation. You must memorize tie-downs so they become a natural part of your presentation. It is imperative to seamlessly flow the ending of your presentation to the final closing sequence. When you use tie-downs, you've already gotten agreements from your client, so it's just one little step more to reach that final agreement. The closing becomes the last of several agreements between you and your client.

Instead of just making statements, follow your statements with a tie-down. Here are some examples:

This car sure handles nicely, *doesn't it?*

This kitchen is a woman's dream, *don't you agree?*

Good health is important, *right?*

Working as hard as you do, you deserve this swimming pool in your back yard. *Isn't that true?*

Listening to tapes keeps you motivated. *Don't you agree?*
These mini-blinds fit this room perfectly, *don't they?*
The slope of this lot is perfect for the house you want to build, *correct?*
The previous owners of this boat sure took good care of it, *didn't they?*
You are mostly concerned with the warranty of our product, *aren't you?*
You can see how simple the maintenance of this hot tub would be, *can't you?*

It is amazing how often I use these everyday, not just in selling but in normal conversations. For several years after my wife and I met, we had a problem because every time I asked a question, I followed it with a tie-down. She would say, "I am not one of your clients; quit trying to sell me." I finally got through to her that I was not selling her. It was just a response that was built into my mind. Now after being around me all these years, she uses tie-downs as much as I do, and our children use them every day, as well. They have heard us use them so many times, tie-downs are a part of their questions. My daughters Jamie and Linzi will say, "Dad, we are going to the lake today, right?" "Dad, you're taking me bowling today, correct?" "Mom, you said we could go to the mall to get my shorts today, didn't you?" "Mom, we need to get my violin fixed, don't we?"

By making these tie-downs part of your everyday walking and talking conversation, you will become a great closer.

You can use reverse tie-downs to give the presentation a relaxed feeling. Reverse tie-downs do not come off as rigid as regular tie-downs to some prospects. The reverse tie-down simply reverses the order of the statement and question. The following are examples of effective reverse tie-downs:

Aren't you happy we have a warranty that covers all these items?

Can't you just see the look on her face when she gets this ring?

Doesn't it make sense that you and your family deserve it?

Don't you agree that it only makes sense to have this entertainment system in your game room?

Haven't they done a fabulous job of planning this subdivision?

Hasn't she done a great job of designing these clothes?

Isn't it amazing how many people overlook safety when they are looking for a car?

Isn't it true that we measure distance by time, not by miles?

Depending on the prospect and situation, one tie-down might be more effective than the other. A combination of both makes for an excellent presentation. Practice on both, so you can use them at anytime on a regular basis. With repetition these questions become fluid.

It's absolutely essential that you memorize these tie-downs so they are a natural part of your conversation. One way you can achieve this is to tape your sales presentation. Then listen to the tape, and everywhere you can use a tie-down, make a note of it. Then tape yourself again with the tie-downs included, and play the tape back every day. If you do this, tie-downs will become entrenched in your mind, and your sales will increase dramatically.

It's important to use different tie-downs and to avoid using the same one over and over, which makes your presentation sound canned. The following is a list of tie-downs that should be memorized and rehearsed:

Aren't they
Aren't we
Aren't you
Can't it
Can't they
Can't you
Correct
Couldn't it
Couldn't they
Couldn't we
Didn't it
Doesn't it

Don't they
Don't we
Don't you agree
Hasn't he
Hasn't she
Haven't they
Isn't it
Isn't that right
Isn't that true
Wasn't it
Won't it
Won't they
Won't you

8

HANDLING OBJECTIONS

Objections reveal the information we need in order to close, and without this information we cannot close. The key is to know how to handle this part of the sales process. Once you have learned and mastered how to handle objections, you will love them; you'll actually look forward to them! There is a real simple formula for closing sales: *objections = sale, no objections = no sale.* Only one objection can prevent a sale from being closed, and the nice thing about this objection is you rarely ever hear it. This objection is a flat out "NO!"

When we ask a customer to buy our product, we usually get one of the following objections in response:

I never make an instant decision

I can't afford it.

I want to think about it.

I have to talk to someone.

I'm just looking.

These objections actually mask the customers' real feelings. They're crying out for more information. You have to dig for more information to get to what the customers are really saying. Once the real objection surfaces, you can close the sale. If it doesn't surface and you don't have the tenacity to find it, your clients will walk out the door without buying from you. They might end up with the same product, but it will be from a competitor who did the job necessary to close the sale.

By agreeing with the client's objections, you make the customers feel important. You are affirming that they have made a good decision. You are telling them it is the same decision you would make if the shoe were on the other foot. After hearing this, they view you as a human being, not as a salesperson. They are saying to themselves, "This person is trying to help, not pressure, me." You cannot disagree by saying:

You can afford it.

You don't have to think about it.

You don't have to talk to someone.

You don't have to look around.

These responses insult the customer' intelligence. Always agree and empathize with the customers. For example, you can use these emphathetic and trust-building responses:

I agree and would never want you to make a decision you are not sure of.

You are wise. I agree that you do need to consider your finances.

I agree with you and appreciate what you are saying. You should think about it.

That's natural and I agree. You should talk with someone.

I can identify with that, and I agree with you. You should look around.

By turning the initial objection around, we can bring out the real objection, which is the area we have to hone in on.

You cannot argue with the clients or make them feel wrong or stupid. If you do, a brick wall will come back up. All the friendship and trust you have built will be destroyed. Who wants to go back to square one? Always agree and empathize; then turn the objection around.

If you give the customers the chance, they will close themselves. Ask questions. You have to keep digging for more details. When you go to doctors for medical problems, the first thing they do is ask questions about this and that. If they don't, where would they start? When taking your car in for mechanical problems, what is the first thing the mechanics do? They ask what is wrong with your car. What is it doing? The same is true in our business. We have to find the problems before we can offer the solution

You must know in advance the objections that are going to be raised and be prepared to overcome them. Always remember to empathize and listen. Ask for the information you need to close the sale. In the next section of the book, we discuss the various closes you can use.

ONLY
CLOSERS
65
make
BIG
MONEY

PART 3: THE CLOSE

My best friend, Mark J. McDonnell, has a saying, "If salespeople do not learn how to close, they might as well buy a mirror so they can watch themselves go broke." Hard core? Yes, but so true.

9

INTRODUCTORY CLOSES

I can provide all the closes in the world to help you sell your product. I can show you different techniques to use when closing, but unless you have sold your product throughout the beginning of your presentation (the front end), all these techniques will not do a bit of good. Your customer has to have some interest in your product before all the closes in the universe can help. You have to find or build desire in your customer before closing.

The great salespeople spend most of their time on the front end, and the closing takes care of itself. By this I mean you find or build desire, then value, for your product, then you fulfill the desire, and then you close. If the three objectives prior to closing are not accomplished, a sale cannot and will not be made. You have to spend the time it takes to get to the close.

There is a danger in closing too soon. There is a right and a wrong time to close. If you try to close too early, you will lose the sale. You have to walk before you run, don't you? You need gas in your car before it will start, don't you agree? You eat a steak after it is cooked, correct? The same principle applies to sales. If you close before your prospect is primed, kiss the sale good-bye.

Going for the kill too early will defeat you. Credibility in yourself, your company, and most of all in your product has to be established before beginning the close.

My wife and I decided to invest in a hot tub. We started looking at different ones on the market. We had a pretty good feel for what we wanted after a few days of looking around. We met a young salesman who knew what we wanted, and he started the onslaught. Within an hour we knew about him, his company, and the difference between hot tubs on the market and the tub he decided to sell us. He explained the difference in jets, pumps, and water lines. We learned about insulation and understood why they could offer the warranty they did. The value of his product outweighed all the others. He made sure the value surpassed his competitions' value. He just flat out gave us a better presentation than anyone else. I guess you know the end of this story, don't you? We own a wonderful spa and are happy we do. We could have spent money on another brand. If after time we had found that the hot tub did not perform up to our needs and expectations, we would have been very unhappy. Building value is the key to closing. Great salespeople spend most of their time setting up the close by doing the things covered in earlier chapters. We have to be in line at all times during the demonstration to make the sale. The closing then takes very little time and makes our job much easier.

The ability to close a sale is an integral part of selling. The fulfillment it gives a salesperson is unsurpassed. It is the feather in one's cap, the triumph, the finishing touch to the total performance. When people in the sales profession reach the point of knowing how to close, they have made the change from common salespeople to great salespeople. If they don't know how to close, full success, total accomplishment, victory will never be theirs. Until you learn this art, you are wasting your time in this profession. Either master it or get out of sales. Do something that does not take as much work and effort. You will be further ahead in the long run. I am not trying to scare you, but it is a fact of life. You can be personable, persuasive, and friendly, which are all essential parts of being a salesperson, but if you do not learn to close, you will never be a great salesperson. Closing is what pays the bills, buys nice houses, clothes, cars, and puts your children through college. The whole sales process demands it and is lost without it. This feat has to be executed or the full rewards of the profession will never be achieved.

POSITIVE STATEMENT CLOSE

Positive Statement closes should be used whenever possible throughout the presentation. They are used to open the mind. As sales professionals, it's our job to open our prospects' minds so they can benefit from our product. Here are several examples of Positive Statement closes:

"*It makes sense* to have the adequate amount of coverage to protect your family's future. Doesn't it?"

"*It's obvious you* would like to invest in the property if we could work out the financing. Isn't that true?"

"This type of advertising *would definitely benefit* your company. Isn't that right?"

"It's *apparent* this brand of carpet suits your living room best. Correct?"

"*You can see how* this type of advertising would increase your sales. Can't you?"

"*There is no doubt* any company that does the volume you do needs a computer system that has all these features. Isn't that true?"

"*It's very clear* to people who work hard for their money that they deserve to drive a luxury car like this. Isn't it?"

"*It is evident* you and your family will have many enjoyable weekends on this boat. Don't you agree?"

Buzzwords like those italicized in these closing statements give the statement more power. The more dominance we can assert, the more authority we command. These words can sway the prospect to see the situation our way. These positive words should be used in every sales call.

DECISION-MAKER CLOSE

This close is commonly used when selling high-ticket items. The person who makes the decision to buy an expensive item is almost impossible to speak with, which poses a big problem for salespeople. Let us examine this situation in detail.

Let's say we are trying to sell an airplane to a company that is spending too much on commercial travel for its employees, but the person who will actually make the decision won't talk to us. He is just too busy and does not have the time, and we cannot get past the steel curtain (who is usually the secretary). Do we go to the next sales call and forget this one, or dig in and conquer the situation?

People in decision-making positions often don't have the time to talk to everybody. That is why they have associates, or *gatekeepers*, who do the preliminary leg work such as gathering facts, details, and price. Our strategy is to get in front of the gatekeeper who can get us in front of the decision-maker. During the presentation, we hit on the highlights of the product, and more importantly, we get the gatekeeper emotionally involved and excited so he or she will sell the appointment for us. We don't take any shortcuts when giving this presentation. The last thing we do is go through the benefits of owning our product. We give the best presentation we're capable of giving, *but we leave out asking for the order*. Why ask the gatekeeper if he or she is not going to make the final decision?

All we want is an appointment with the decision-maker, and the gatekeeper is vital to getting us that appointment. This individual will benefit by getting credit for setting up such a valuable appointment that led to a wise decision being made. You will be surprised at how many appointments you can get by tying personal advancement to the right individual. Never underestimate the influence of the gatekeeper. This person has a sense of loyalty to the company and the decision-maker, and when the sale is consummated, this person will have a feeling of satisfaction. This person will feel that he or she has made the final decision. We all have egos, and people in this position have a strong ego drive. As individuals climb the corporate ladder, the stronger this drive gets.

Some people will read this and say, "Why should I have to give two presentations to sell the product?" In high-ticket sales giving two presentations is sometimes a necessity. If you give the presentation over the phone, you are making a serious mistake that could cost you thousands of dollars in commissions. This is a shortcut that great salespeople never make.

CONQUERING-THE-OBLIGATION CLOSE

If you feel sympathetic for every excuse a prospect tells you, your sales career is in deep jeopardy. Conquering-the-obligation close is one of the most powerful closes I can share with you. Let's say your prospects tell you they would love to buy your product but need to pay money to the IRS. Well, if you have ever been in that situation or know someone who has, and you let sympathy enter into the sale, you lose. If you start thinking, "Boy, I've been there before. I know I had to pay them everything I could get my hands on, and I know they cannot afford this right now," you lose. If you believe in your product and feel that the prospects will benefit by owning it, they have been cheated if you don't sell it to them.

You conquer the obligation by saying with empathy, "I can appreciate your situation and fully understand. Let me ask you a question. Other than the IRS, is there any reason you would not take advantage of this situation today?" If they say that's the only reason, close with this question, "Taking into consideration your IRS problems, how much could you put toward this?" Conquer the obligation, and you will find some money for your product. You have to separate the two.

This close will work for all products, and more importantly, it will conquer any excuse for not buying the product today. Other excuses can come up. I call them "excuses," because that is exactly what they are until you turn them around into a sale. Let's say your prospect tells you that he and his wife have been saving money for a trip to Hawaii. Well, let me tell you something, those people deserve to go to Hawaii. It might be the only time in their lives they can go, and they deserve it. Do not try to convince them not to do something they have been thinking about doing all their lives. They deserve it, and chances are you won't convince them not to. If you try to persuade them not to go, all the trust and friendship you have built is thrown out the window.

Instead, empathize, and tell them you wouldn't do anything to keep them from going. You could say "Taking into consideration the fact that you are going to Hawaii, and I am not going to do anything to keep you from that because you deserve it. How much could you put towards this?"

Let's look at another example. Here's another obligation that a prospect might bring up, "I would like to have this policy, but right now I'm saving money because my daughter is starting college next year." Your response is "I recognize the problem you have and certainly can identify with it. If you had had a policy like this for her while she was growing up, you wouldn't have to worry about it now. Would you? Well, you have two younger children that you are going to have the same problem with. Aren't you? To keep from having this same situation come up again, doesn't it make sense to prevent it now if it is at all possible? Taking into account that your daughter will be starting college next year, how much could you put towards this, so you won't have to deal with it again?" You have to empathize and agree that the clients should do what they already planned to do. Then separate and conquer the obligation. You will make more money and, more important, it will make your prospects happier.

People in all walks of life have obligations or needs they have to deal with. Just because they have them doesn't mean they can't consider your product. But if you sympathize with these people, you will always lose a sale, and more importantly, your prospects lose because you have not serviced their needs. Empathize but never sympathize. The key to this close is to help the client handle the original obligation.

YEAH! YEAH! CLOSE

When no objections are brought up during the presentation, many salespeople get all excited and think they definitely have a sale. They are thinking, "Oh boy, they love it, they want it, they are going to buy it." Ha! Without objections there will never be a sale. I guess I should never say "never." Put another way, the chances are 99.99 percent the sale is lost. If the client doesn't ask any questions or has no objections during your presentation, you have a huge problem. They are giving you the Yeah! Yeah! You better back up, and start asking more questions yourself. Get the prospect more involved. If you don't, your closing percentage will be the remainder of 99.99 percent, which means you will be in another profession very soon.

Here's how to get the parents and children more involved when dealing with a family. First direct these questions to the parents, "From your actions, I can see you folks really like the benefits of my product, right? You can also see the benefits it will give the entire family, correct?" Then direct this question to the kids, "I'm sure you kids will enjoy it, won't you?" Kids can and will put pressure on their parents.

Another way to handle this when working with just husband and wife is to ask, "What do you like most about our product?" The prospect will respond in one of two ways. They will tell you what they like and you can close, or they will say, "Oh, we like it, but we can't buy today." You can follow the latter response with this, "I can appreciate what you are saying. From your reactions I assume you folks would like to own our product." Then look dumbfounded, "Can I ask you something? It's obvious you like our product, right?" They have to say "yes." "You can definitely see the value. Can't you?" Again, they have to say "yes." You say, "The benefits for your family are without question. We already know that, don't we? Can you help me with one thing so I can share it with my next customer?" Now they think they are off the hook, and they have to say "yes." "What about our product doesn't fit your needs today?" Now they have to tell you the objections so you can close the sale. Now you are doing the Yeah! Yeah!

The objections could be many different reasons, but at least now you have the chance to overcome these objections. Without hearing them you are sunk. Great salespeople know that and look forward to these objections.

Sometimes all these questions might not be necessary to get to the close. But using this last one tells us what the customers don't like, and we should be able to overcome these objections. Many salespeople won't take the time or energy to handle this situation. The Yeah! Yeah! is a red flag, and they don't want to deal with this problem. The great salespeople will love it. Remember, turn the Yeah! Yeah! into a closing sequence, and your income will increase dramatically. Yeah! Yeah! Yeah!

10

SHARP ANGLE CLOSES

These closes are the most powerful of all. They are also the most dangerous. If these closes are not used at the proper time, the client will run faster than an Olympic Gold Medalist. The brick wall we knocked down in the warmup will reappear, and the sale will be lost. Many salespeople use these closes from beginning to end. Wrong! These closes are to be used when our presentation is near the end, and we've come down to just one or two objections. We should know by the objections during the presentation when this moment arrives. Let's look at some examples.

The following illustrate the Sharp Angle closes in response to questions that clients ask:

"Does this car come with an extended warranty?"

"*If* it does, would you like to own it?"

"Does this computer have the capability of producing labels?"

"*If* I can include that in the package, do you want it?"

"Does the price of the boat include the trailer?"

"*If* I can include the trailer, do you want it?"

"Does this suit include alterations?"

"*If* we can alter it at no cost, do you want it?"

REVERSE SHARP ANGLE CLOSE

In the Reverse Sharp Angle, you simply reverse the order of the statement and question:

"Does the TV come with the stand?"

"Do you want the TV *if* I can include the stand?"

"Does the cost for advertising include setup and full color processing?"

"Would you like to advertise with us *if* I can get it included?"

"Is the padding for the carpet in that price?"

"Would you like us to install this carpet in your house *if* the padding is included?"

"Do you guarantee if I switch over to your phone system it will save me money?"

"Will you switch over *if* I can guarantee it?"

TAKE AWAY SHARP ANGLE CLOSE

In the Take Away Sharp Angle close, you demonstrate a little hesitation about the product having the features the client asks for. This creates a psychological effect of making the client want the product even more. It's as if you're taking it away. For example, suppose the client asks, "Does this price include free delivery?" You respond, "Not always; although, if we have another delivery in your area, we might be able to get it to you at no cost. *If* we can do this, do you want it?"

Client: "Does this pool table come with a cover?"

Salesperson: "It comes with balls, cues, and a rack. Some of our tables do include a cover. Let me check to see if this is one of them. Do you want the table *if* I can include a cover?"

Client: "Does this lawn mower come with a grass catcher?"

Salesperson: "Not that I'm aware of, but let me find out. *If* we can include it in the cost, would you like to own it?"

Client: "Does the cool decking come with the swimming pool?"

Salesperson: "There's usually an extra charge for the decking, but since the ground doesn't appear to have a lot of rock it will be easier to dig. In that case we might be able to include it in the total cost. Would you like the pool *if* we could include the decking at no cost?"

ASSUMPTION/ACTION SHARP ANGLE CLOSE

In this close, you implicitly ask the client to assume the product has the feature they want and then follow with a closing question that makes the client act. Here are some examples:

Client: "Does this car come with an extended warranty?"

Salesperson: "I think it does but I'm not sure. I'll have to check. *If* it does, how soon do you need it *delivered*?"

Client: "Does this suit include alterations?"

Salesperson: "Not usually. We have to send them out to another tailor because we're so backed up. But *if* I can get it done at no cost, how soon would you like to *pick* it up?"

Client: "Does this computer have the capability of producing labels?"

Salesperson: "*If* I can include that in the package, how soon do you need me to come out, *set* it up, and *train* your office staff?"

Client: "Does the cool decking come with the swimming pool?"

Salesperson: "There's usually an extra charge for the decking, but since the ground doesn't appear to have a lot of rock and it will be easy to dig, we might be able to include it in the cost. *If* I can include the decking, how soon do you want the pool *completed*?"

COLUMBO SHARP ANGLE CLOSE

Some TV shows contribute a lot to the sales profession. I love to watch a real closer in action, and Columbo is without a doubt the absolute best. His technique is great. Think about it. He asks questions and more questions, and then walks away. But just before he leaves, he turns around and says, "Excuse me, but can I ask you just one more question?" He does this throughout the investigation until he gets the guilty person. What a closer! He's a master at work! Let's see how this approach can be of value to salespeople.

Let's say a client asks, "Does the price include free delivery?" You respond with "Not always. Although if we have another delivery in your area we might be able to get it to you at no cost. I'll have to check my manifest to see if we have anything coming out your way." Now get up, and start walking out to check your manifest. Stop! Turn around, and Columbo: "Let me ask you this. *If* we can get it delivered at no cost, do you want it?"

Or suppose the client asks, "Does this pool table come with a cover?" You respond with "It comes with balls, cues, and a rack. Some tables include covers. Let me see if this one does." Get up, and start walking away. Stop! Turn around, and Columbo: "*If* we can include the cover, do you want it?"

If the client asks, "Does this lawnmower come with a grass catcher?" you respond with "Not that I'm aware of, but let me find out." Start to walk away. Stop! Turn around, and

Columbo: "*If* we can include the grass catcher, would you like to own it?"

Client: "Does the cool decking come with the swimming pool?" You: "There's usually an extra charge for the decking, but since the ground doesn't appear to have a lot of rock, it will be easier to dig. In that case, we might be able to include it in the total cost. Can I use your phone to find out for you?" Get up to use the phone, assuming you are in their home. Stop! Turn around, and Columbo: "Would you like the pool *if* we could include the decking at no cost?"

The key is the Columbo. You have to stop, turn around, put a hand to your forehead or chin, and ask the question. Remember, great salespeople sometimes have to be actors.

THE SMOKE-OUT SHARP ANGLE CLOSE

We use this close to elicit the final and last objection or objections to the close. Again, it has to be done as described and should be carried out with *finesse.*

I call this close the "smoke-out" because that is what we are doing—smoking out the final objection or objections.

To illustrate this close, let's use some examples of the previous closes we've discussed:

Sharp Angle

"Does this car come with an extended warranty?"

"Other than the extended warranty is there anything else that would stop you from driving this car home today?"

If "no," close with: "*If* it does, would you like to own it?"

Reverse Sharp Angle

"Does the cost for advertising included set-up and full color processing?"

"Is there anything besides the set-up and full color processing that would keep you from advertising with us?" If "no," close with: "Would you like to advertise with us *if* I can get it included?

Take Away Sharp Angle

"Does the lawn mower come with a grass catcher?"

"Not that I'm aware of, but let me find out. Besides the grass catcher is there anything else that would keep you from taking it with you today?" If "no," close with: "Would you like the mower *if* we can include the grass catcher?"

Assumption/Action Sharp Angle

"Does the computer have the capacity of producing labels?"

"In addition to the labels, is there any other reason you wouldn't want the computer?" If "no," close with: "*If* I can include that in the package, how soon do you need me to come out, *set* it up and *train* your office staff?"

Columbo Sharp Angle

"Does the price include free delivery?"

"Not always! Although if we have another delivery in your area we might be able to get it to you at no cost. I'll have to check our manifest to see if we have one coming your way." Now, get up and start walking out to check your manifest. Stop! Turn around and Columbo: "Other than the delivery, is there anything else that would keep you from going ahead?" If "no," close with: "*If* we can do this, do you want it?"

In these examples, we have learned how to close if the answer is "no." What if the answer is "yes"? If the client's answer is "yes," you have another objection or question. You overcome this objection, and then go back to the one you originally closed on. For example, suppose the client asks, "Does the TV come with the stand?" You respond with "Other than the stand is there anything else that would keep you from taking it home today?"

"Yes. How long is the warranty?"

"It comes with a two-year warranty, which include parts and labor. Anything else?"

If the client's answer is "no," close with this, "*If* we can include the stand would you like to take it with you?"

You can see why it is important to know where you are in the presentation before using this close. You have to be down to the last one or two objections. If you're not, the brick wall will appear, and you have serious problems.

In some cases, you have to quote a price a little higher than the bottom line to include some of the extra items. Again, every product has four or five of the same objections. When you find out which ones they are, you will know how much to raise your product price depending on the cost of such items.

You will notice I've emphasized *if* in many of the examples. Never doubt the power of this one statement: to a great salesperson, a true closer, "if" is the biggest word in the dictionary.

"*If* I could, would you?" "Would you, *if* I could?" "Obviously you would like to own it, *if* I could?" *If, if,* and *if* some more.

The Sharp Angle closes must be practiced before being used. Take a look at your product, and decide which Sharp Angle closes to implement in your presentation. These closes cut to the chase, and go right for the sale, and that is why they are so dangerous. If you use them too early, your prospect will run. When used after the customer is sold on your product and is down to one or two objections, these closes can get your sale immediately. Timing is the key. Use these closes with care, and your sales will increase by leaps and bounds.

11

BRING BACK THE HAMBURGER AND OTHER CLOSES

This close is used when prospects have to discuss owning your product with their spouses for a short period of time. They might say, "I like your product. My wife and I are going to have a bite to eat, and we'll talk it over." What reason do they have to come back if they decide not to buy your product? None whatsoever, correct? You have a slim chance of selling these people if they don't come back. Would you rather them come back every time or try to sell them over the phone? Your closing percentage will definitely be higher when you are in front of them.

Remember, most people don't like salespeople. If they have made up their minds not to buy your product, there is no reason to come back to tell you they have decided not to go ahead with the sale. They feel if they do, the high pressure will start taking place. If you can get them back, even if their answer is "no," you have an opportunity to overcome any of their objections. Here's how you can get them to come back.

" We'd like to go have a bite to eat and talk it over."

"Great! Could you do me a big favor? We've been so busy today I haven't had a chance to eat a thing. I won't have any chance of getting away at all. Could you bring me back a hamburger?"

Always take money out of your pocket, and hand it to them. This is an absolute must. If they won't take it, insist that they do. Many times they will say, "I'll be happy to pick it up and take care of it for you," but don't ever let this happen. Always demand that they take the money. If you have to, put the money in the husband's shirt pocket. If they don't take your money, chances are they won't show up even though they say they will. If they have your money, they will always come back with your food. This gives you that extra chance to close them. If you are selling a product where your average commission is $400 and you get ten more sales a year, that is $4,000. Your out-of-pocket hamburger money is very small compared to your return on investment. In Chapter 2 when I was describing great salespeople, I stated that great salespeople will spend their own money to succeed. This close is one example of just that. Not everyone who comes back will buy your product. But a higher percent who come back will buy than those who do not come back. This I can guarantee.

SECONDARY QUESTION/MAJOR-MINOR CLOSE

This close is used at the back end of the presentation. It is a major question *immediately* followed by a minor question that can finalize the sale. When clients answer the minor question they have committed themselves. The minor commitments bring us closer to the sale. Let's look at some examples. In each example, you'll notice that it's important not to pause and to keep talking.

"Do you prefer the blue or white upholstery? (Don't stop.) By the way, will you take me water skiing some weekend?"

"Do you want to pick it up on Thursday or Friday? (Don't stop.) I've got a better idea. How about if I deliver it personally?"

"Would you like your first vacation in the Caribbean or Hawaii? (Don't stop.) Incidentally, will you send me a post card?"

"Do you prefer the four or six person hot tub? (Don't stop.) By the way, who's going to be the first to use it?"

This gets the clients to make a minor decision, and once they answer this question the major decision has been made. I have told you to shut up after asking a closing question. Right? In this close we should shut up after asking the second question. If the close is not done in this manner, the heart of it is taken away. We do shut up, but only at the right moment. Another way of using this close is as follows:

"Do you prefer the blue or white upholstery? (Don't stop.) By the way, will you take me water skiing some weekend?"

"Sure. "

"Would the blue or the white upholstery be better?"

"Do you want to pick up your stereo system on Thursday or Friday? (Don't stop.) I've got a better idea. How about if I deliver it personally?"

"Fine."

Would Thursday or Friday be better?"

"Would you like your first vacation in the Caribbean or Hawaii? (Don't stop.) Incidentally, will you send me a post card?"

"Of course."

"Great. Would you prefer the Caribbean or Hawaii?"

"Do you prefer the four or six person hot tub? (Don't stop.) By the way, who's going to be the first to use it?"

"Both of us."

"Great. Would the four or six person tub fit your needs?"

By using this technique, you have the clients answer the minor question followed by answering the major question. Questions, questions, questions. Commitments, commitments, commitments. The combination of both of these is the key to closing the sale.

ALTERNATE-OF-CHOICE CLOSE

This close is used to pin the prospects down. Every question asked when using this close puts our prospects in the buying mode. When they answer each question, they have made a minor commitment to buy our product. Just as when eating an orange, we peel it first, and we throw the peeling away and eat the orange inside. In sales, alternate-of-choice questions get to the important issues. We ask our prospects a question or questions so that they have to give a response to two choices. Whichever they choose brings us closer to a sale. Either answer is a positive move to the close. The one they did not choose for the answer is like the orange peeling we discarded. It now has no influence towards making the sale.

This close gets to the meat of the sale. It helps us decide what product in our product line we're going to sell our prospects. It can create urgency by eliminating the unimportant obstacles. Alternative options narrow down the field. When we get to this point, the sale falls into place almost naturally. Let's look at a few examples.

"Obviously you'd like the pool installed as soon possible. Correct? Would you like us to start digging Wednesday or would Thursday be better?"

"Can I help you?"

"Yes, I'm looking for a suit."

"Well, from looking at you, I would say you wear a 44 long or a 46 regular."

"I wear a 44 long."

"Great. Let me show you what we have in your size. Are you looking for a particular color?"

"Gray."

"Light or dark?"

Here's another example:

"I'd like to look at your health club facilities."

"Great. Have you looked at any other clubs in town?"

"Yes."

"Which ones?"

"Well, let me show you around. Are you looking to firm up or increase your cardiovascular stamina?"

These closes put the prospects on the spot. These are excellent to use when making appointments on the phone. "Hello. This is David Plummer with XYZ Company. We have a new product we've just come out with. It would definitely increase your volume when used in addition to what you already have with us. I'd like to come out and spend ten to fifteen minutes to show how it can increase productivity. Would Tuesday or Wednesday be better?"

"Tuesday."

"Morning or afternoon?"

"Morning."

"Would 9:00 work into your schedule or would 10:00 be better?"

"9:00."

"Good. I'll see you then. Have a great day."

12

VERBAL BEN AND OTHER CLOSES

Most people don't realize that Ben Franklin had the uncanny ability to make right decisions, not only in his personal life but also in business. He would break down each decision and weigh the plusses and minuses. More importantly, though, he never deviated from this method and always lived with the one choice that outweighed the other. He would draw a large T on a piece of paper. On the left, he wrote down the minuses (or why he should not), and on the right, he wrote down the plusses (or why he should). This made his decision-making simple.

The Ben Franklin close has been used for decades as a way of showing people the plusses and minuses of owning a product. Of course, it is always best to have more plusses than minuses to close the sale. Obviously the salesperson can provide the plusses. When you encounter customers that can't make their mind about your product, suggest that they write down why they should and should not own the product, starting with why they should not.

For example, they could create a list like the one that follows:

Why I should not	Why I should
Initial investment	Investment opportunity
Kid's college	Use
Uncertain	Security
	Tax write-off
	Family's future
	Self accomplishment

The problem with this close is that it has been used forever. As salespeople, we have to constantly make adjustments, because your customers know this close as well as you do. When you start to use it, a red flag goes up in the customers' minds. Don't get me wrong. It is a great close. However, there's a way to use this close without the customers' putting up a red flag. It is the Verbal Ben.

"I'm sure you have reasons why you would not or could not get involved with us today and obvious reasons why you should. Correct?" What can they say to this? They have to answer "yes." You continue, "So I can better understand your situation, could you first give me the reasons why you would not or could not, and then why you should." (Don't stop.) "The reason I would like to know is because it will help me with future clients like yourselves. Why could you not get involved?" Wait until they give you two reasons, then stop them.

"Hold on just one minute so I can write these down." Start writing them down, and then go to the reasons why they should get involved. When they run out of reasons, help them with reasons you have covered in the presentation and get them to agree with these reasons. Always make sure to have twice as many reasons why they should get involved. Once the list is completed, turn the paper around and say, "It's pretty obvious there are more reasons to get involved than not, right?" At this point they can either buy your product or give you an objection to close on.

The difference between the standard Ben Franklin and the Verbal Ben is that with the Verbal Ben the customer is helping to eliminate a red flag. If you go through the standard Ben by telling them about Ben Franklin and his ability to make decisions, you are giving away the power of the Verbal Ben. Don't say or do anything to tip them off. You just ask them the reasons they should and should not buy your product. Instead of their writing down the reasons, you get them to tell these reasons to you, and then you stop them and start writing these reasons down as if these are for your personal reference. This is an excellent close to use in response to the "I want to think about it" objection.

Kids' Close

Kids can be a salesperson's best friend. The fact is children do not take "no" very well. They never have; they never will. How many times have you become irritated at your own children for asking "why" when you say "no"? Many times, right? Since this is an accepted fact, why don't we use it to our advantage? Since it can help us make more sales, we should, shouldn't we?

Many so-called salespeople do not want to deal with kids during their presentation. If they would learn how to use the kids to their benefit, they would make a lot more money. So take advantage of this closing tool whenever possible. Use everything to your advantage.

A good friend told me about a sales meeting he conducted. Some of his salespeople were complaining about people bringing children to the sales presentations. They wanted to tell potential clients they should get a babysitter for the youngsters and leave them at home before coming to view the property being sold. The top salesperson in his organization stood up and said he would take all the clients with kids so the others would not have to deal with this problem. He then explained how he sold such a high percentage of these people: he included the kids in the presentation. He made them part of the decision-making process.

When showing the property, he made sure to include the kids in different situations. When showing the amenities (such as swimming pools, tennis courts, fishing docks, etc.), he directed questions at the kids about how much fun they would have using these facilities. Pretty soon the kids were closing the parents. He let the children do all the selling. His logic was perfect because kids don't take "no" very well. They won't stop asking for the order. If your product relates at all to kids, they can be your best ally. The greatest part of this close is that the salesperson is the good guy. You are not applying any pressure. The kids are putting on more pressure than you ever could. If you are selling a product where kids can be helpful, use them.

A good illustration involves my own son. As we all know once kids start asking, you will continue to hear about it until they are blue in the face or your ear drums can't take anymore—more than likely, both. My son, Roger, called me at my office one day to see if he could get new tennis shoes. In today's world a pair of high-flying, double-bouncing, let-me-look-cool-to-my-friends footwear can cost in excess of a hundred dollars. Whatever happened to the days of a $20 to $25 dollar pair of sneakers? That might be good enough for us, but not for some kids today. They have to look cool to their buddies.

I told my son if I was going to spend that kind of money for a pair of shoes, I wanted the lowest possible price. I said, "Roger, I'll tell you what I'll do. I want you to do a market survey. Get out the phone book and call every place in town that sells these tennis shoes, and I'll buy them. Maybe they are on sale someplace, and old Dad can save a few bucks. I don't want to have to pay any more that I have to when we're talking this kind of money." I thought he'll never sit down and take the time to do the research. I thought I had him this time, that I was off the hook. As our kids sometimes say, "No way!"

He called me back a few hours later to inform me of the good, or should I say bad, news. He found a place that had the tennis shoes for ten dollars less than anybody else in town. Here is how the conversation went.

"Dad, guess what?" As I slumped in my chair, he continued, "I got us a great deal." (I'm thinking, a great deal for whom, him or me?) "Dad, are you still there?"

"Yeah, Rog, I'm still here."

"I found a place that can save us a bunch of money. They are ten dollars less than any other place in town."

"Okay, Rog, how many places did you call?" As I look back, I don't know why I ever asked this dumb question. I was a cooked goose. He proceeded to run off the names of ten to fifteen places in town.

"Dad?"

"Yeah, Rog."

"They only had one pair left in my size. I told them to hold them for me. We have to be there by 5:00. They can't hold them past then. What time can you be home to pick me up?"

What could I say to that sales presentation? He did exactly what I asked him to do. His urgency to act now was infectious, and he had asked the closing question. By 5:15 he was wearing those new tennis shoes. Our offspring can be absolutely relentless at times. Kids can and will close the sale. Get these children helping you sell the parents.

TAKE 'EM BACK, THEN BRING 'EM BACK CLOSES

Some products can be sold by the salesperson illustrating what benefits can be obtained by making a decision today based on a comparable situation in the past. These closes are used to place the clients in a situation where they look at the past and have a chance to do something now they wish they had done then. We have all looked at opportunities that came our way only to pass them up and wish we had taken advantage of them when they were presented to us. How many times have we looked at something that was on sale at a tremendous discount, only to go back at a later date and find the same item at double the cost? Many, many times. We cannot dwell on the past; we can only use past experiences as learning tools for the future. Right? Since we know that everyone learns from the past, why not use past experiences as closing tools? All we have to do is relate the present opportunity to a past or missed opportunity and close the sale. Sometimes we have to be very blunt and almost intimidating when explaining the benefits. Let's see how these two closes work; then take a look at your product to see if it would work for you.

TIME MACHINE CLOSE

How many times have you driven past an area and said, "If we'd only invested in that property five years ago when we had the opportunity," or "If we'd bought that house back then," or "If I'd only taken advantage of what the insurance premiums were when I was twenty-five." Once you put the prospects into the past situation when they had a similar opportunity and get them to agree that this has happened to them, continue with the following:

"Well, let's say we are in a time machine, and I have the ability to turn back the time to again give you the opportunity to take advantage of the premiums at that cost. You would take advantage of it in a second. Wouldn't you? Of course you would! Now then, consider the facts here in front of you. The same opportunity is here today. If you don't take advantage of this opportunity now, you will be looking back again wishing you had, and we both know you don't want to look back again, don't we? Let's get you started."

PAST, PRESENT AND FUTURE CLOSE

Clients often say, "I like everything about your program. When I get some of my bills paid off, I'll get back with you." We could sympathize and say to ourselves, "Well, I've been there before and can understand why he can't do anything right now."   Most people are always going to have bills to pay, and unless they are helped in making a decision, they will never do anything. If you are selling a good product, don't be ashamed to dig for more information and push a little. In the sales profession you will hear excuses like this all the time. These are not objections, but excuses. Excuses are like bills, most of us have them. We always have; we always will. We could pack up our bags and go home, or respond by saying the following:
"Let's say I was sitting in your home several years ago showing you and your family this same policy. At that time, you had the same response—that you had to pay off some bills before you could do anything. Let's look at how you and your family could have benefited over that time. Your monthly premiums would have been less, and you and your family would have built quite a sound retirement plan. Correct? Right now you would be thanking me for having the foresight to help you and your family. Right? Now let's look at today and see how you and your family can benefit. We're only talking x dollars per month, or x dollars per day. (Break it down to a daily figure.) A few years from now you will be thanking me because you and your family will have a sound future and if

anything should happen to you, heaven forbid, this policy will take care of your family. Not only will you have security for your future retirement and college education for your children, but you will also have the peace of mind that your family will be well taken care of. You see, there are always going to be bills to pay, but let me ask you a question, what really is the most important obligation in your life? Your family, right? Your family deserves it. Don't they? Now if I come back sometime in the future, you are still going to be facing the same problems with maybe different obligations. The premiums will be more, and you will have lost all the money you could have saved towards your retirement and your family's needs. We both know that a few dollars a day isn't going to stand in your way from paying off your bills, don't we? Let's get you started."

You could also show on paper how much money they would have paid in the past and how much they would have saved by today. In addition, show them how much money the policy costs today and how much money they will have saved in the future. A combination of both of these is very effective. Tell them first, and then show them. For example, you can use a table similar to the following:

Past	Today
X dollars per month	X dollars per month or X dollars per day
Today	Future
X dollars saved	X dollars saved

Let's look at what makes this close so powerful. We put the clients in a past situation and make them agree that they have been in this situation. Unless they agree that this has happened, this close will not work. Once they agree, you continue with the close. When they commit to the statement that they would take advantage of the situation or opportunity if you could turn back time, they have bought your product. The clients have admitted they have been there before, they would do what they did not do, and more importantly, they do not want to look back again at a decision they did not make. Again, you have to get them to admit to these mistakes in the past, or this close will not work.

This close is a good one to use when your client cannot make a decision. People need your help in making decisions. They are afraid of making a bad decision so they don't make any decision at all. It is your duty to help these people, or they will end up with nothing. Not wanting to deal with situations in the present, people live in the past. If you are selling a good product, they will be happy you helped them with these decisions. I once read a quote from one of our generals in the armed forces, "More wars have been lost from indecision than wrong decisions." Not making such decisions is not conducive to people's well-being. So help them.

13

ONE DAY CLOSES

TIMESHARE CLOSE

Customers will react in three ways when you ask them to buy:

1. They will buy.
2. They will ask a buying question.
3. They will give you another objection.

If you scrutinize the Timeshare close, you can see I do not always wait for an answer when asking a question with a tie-down, and sometimes I wait for the answer. Why? By responding to the clients' personality and the present situation, I can make the close more powerful.

Let's look at an example of the Timeshare close:

"I agree with you. You should think it over. You should not spend your money on something you would never use or spend it in a place that you might lose it. But at the same time, you should spend your money on those things that will return great benefits, right? You see, you have already thought about it, and making an instant decision is impossible. You've thought about going on vacations before. Correct? You've definitely dreamed of a perfect vacation for you and your family. Haven't you?" (Nod your head up and down when saying "Haven't you?") "You see, you have already thought about it.

You want to make your vacation more valuable for you and your family and be able to visit more places. Don't you? After all what do we work for? Quality time with our families, right? So it makes sense to timeshare your vacation and to guarantee your vacation at today's price forever while enjoying that quality time together. Right? It is impossible to make an instant decision, or do something that you haven't already thought about. Now let me ask you, where would you like to go on your first vacation? Great. Let's get you started. By the way, will you send me a post card?"

In the first paragraph I am building momentum, and I don't want to be stopped with a negative answer before I get started. I need to get the clients in a decision-making mode. Once they realize they have thought about these things before and realize that making an instant decision is impossible, I can start getting answers on minor questions that will be answered with positive answers. This leads people to make a decision.

An adage says, "Never speak after asking a closing question," which I believe wholeheartedly. However, these questions are not designed to be closing questions. These are momentum-building questions to program the clients' mind for the close. If you do not use them properly, your clients will feel pressured into a decision, and that's why cancellations occur. By asking these questions we are seeding the mind with positive information, so when we need the closing questions answered, the right response will come from the prospects.

Most products that are sold on a one-day close have higher cancellation rates than products sold differently. However, these products cannot be sold any other way, or very, very few, if any, sales would be made at all. When selling these products, we have to live with this fact. By mastering these techniques we can limit them to a certain degree. Great salespeople learn this style of closing and make a lot more money than salespeople who don't. Wouldn't you agree this could increase your sales? It is obvious it will, isn't it?

YES/NO CLOSE

Sometimes we cannot get people to make a decision. They are not saying "yes," but they are not giving us a flat out "no" either. Again, if we are selling a good product that fits our clients' needs, it is our job to help them make decisions. In most cases, people do not want to make a bad decision that could possibly affect their lives in a negative way. This is true not only in the sales profession. Doctors, lawyers, accountants, all different professionals, have to help their clients make decisions.

Recently, I had radial keratonomy surgery. I had been considering doing it for years. I spoke with two different eye surgeons, and one asked me a number of questions: What did I expect from the surgery? Why did I want the surgery? Did I not like wearing glasses? Was the surgery for cosmetic reasons? After hearing my answers, he helped me make a decision. I was apprehensive about letting anybody operate on my eyes. After I answered all of his questions, he explained the procedure, and I proceeded to have it done. Selling is really part of all professions and is done in all walks of life. Making sales is the basis of our society. Most everything we do involves persuasion, and the way things are presented helps people make decisions.

Some salespeople say, "I can't get pushy or put pressure on people," but you don't have to. If the sale is presented properly, your prospects will put the pressure on themselves.

At times people are mentally stuck. You just cannot get them to make a decision. They feel in their hearts and minds a bad decision is a "yes" or a "no." They are thinking, "If I don't do this I might regret it, but if I do and it doesn't turn out to be good for me, I'll also regret it. What to do? What to do?" It is our job to help them make the right decision, which is the purpose of the Yes/No close. The following is an example:

"When you leave here tonight you will have made a decision. You will have either told me 'yes' and will participate in the program, or you will tell me 'no.' Let us look at both situations. Let's say you say 'no.' Let's talk about how you will feel when you go home tonight. When you and your wife get home, she will say, 'Honey, you know that was a fantastic program. It would be great to take all those nice vacations at a fixed price for the rest of our lives. The reason we don't vacation now is because every time we plan to go all we talk about is how much it costs, so we never go. What I like about it is it forces us to go some place every year, and that's really nice. Well, I guess we better forget about it. I hope we are not sorry next year when we want to go someplace and it's so expensive we can't go where we want to, and we have to settle for something less like we have in the past.'

"That's what you'll hear if you say 'no.' Now suppose you say 'yes.' When you get home you say to your wife, 'Sweetie, I'm so happy that we finally did something that will force us to go somewhere as a family every year; that will be really nice. We can now go to places we never could go before. I can take you and the kids to places you've always wanted to go. I won't have to worry because it will be prepaid.'

"Folks, these two couples are going home tonight; one wishing and wondering, and the other feeling great. Which one would you rather be? The one who isn't sure, or the one who has a future? Let's get you started."

LOST OPPORTUNITY CLOSE

This close is used when people say they cannot buy your product because they are saving all their disposable income. We all know saving some of our money is very important. However, if we sell a product that can give our customers a better return than what they are currently getting, this close can be very helpful.

For example, you might hear something like this from a client, "I like your program very much. However, at the present time I'm saving my money."

"I agree with you totally. We all need to save some of our money. We need to have something to fall back on, especially in case of an emergency, right? But sometimes we can't see the forest through the trees because all we do is save, save, save. I remember a friend of mine who saved every penny he made. Every time a good opportunity came by that would give him a much better return on his money, he would not listen. He missed out on some excellent opportunities. He will be the first to tell you this. He had the additional money to invest because he saved just like you. Banks love people who put money in savings accounts. The banks pay people interest on their money and then loan it back to them to buy homes, cars, boats, and other things that the banks finance. The banks pay their clients 5 to 6 percent, and then turn around and loan it back to them at 10 to 15 percent. Not a bad situation for the banks, is it? I agree we need to have some of our money in the bank to be liquid. However, based on the return they give, there are better places to put your money from an investment standpoint. Don't you agree? If this investment continues to do what it has done in the past, you can do much better than putting your money in the bank. Makes sense, doesn't it?"

Now the client will buy, ask a buying question, or give you another objection, which at this point in the book, you know how to deal with, right?

GET-IT-ON-THE-TABLE CLOSE

This close is used for the clients who are not going along with you, but who will not give you a reason why. Sometimes it is an objection that has not surfaced. It is in their minds, but they have not put it on the table yet. If you do not get it out, they will leave your office, and you will be wondering why they did not buy your product. If this happens, you have only yourself to blame because you did not do your job in helping them make that decision. People cannot always make a decision based on what you have told them. However, they can make a decision based on new information. It could be one little thing that prevents them from going along with you. In this close, you allow the client to say "no," but every time the client says "no," that client is actually saying "yes."

For example, you say, "Just to clarify my thinking, what exactly is keeping you from getting involved with us? (Don't stop.) Is it the credibility of our company? Is it me personally?" They will say "no" in most cases to these two questions. Then go back over each step of the presentation with one question at a time. Is it this, or is it that? Each time they say "no," you have a "yes." Don't you? Finally, you can get to the objection or objections that are keeping them from making the commitment and deal with that specific objection. (Handling objections is covered in Chapter 8.)

RIP-OFF CLOSE

Many people have experienced bad situations in the past. Something they did or a decision they made at another time that did not work out left a bad taste in their mouths. We can all look back to something we did that did not turn out for the best. However, if we let a bad experience from the past stop us from moving forward, our lives will be pretty dull. We would never move on to bigger and better things. We could never grow mentally or spiritually. We would just be sitting in a negative state of mind for our entire lives. That, my friends, is not a good way to live. It is not fair to teach our children this way of life. We as parents should be teaching our offspring how to handle the downfalls of life, how to bounce back from a bad situation, and go forward for a better life.

In Chapter One, I told you about a gentleman who lost everything when he didn't strike it rich in the gold field. What would have happened if he had stopped trying? That one bad experience would have ruined him for the rest of his life. The horrible fact is that many people do exactly what he did. They stop after one bad situation. This close is designed for people who will not forget a bad situation and move on. This close, my friends, is a powerful and emotional one that works.

Let's say you can't get your clients to make a decision. They are on the fence, and they just won't commit. Finally after all is said and done, it comes out: "I've been ripped off before!"

You respond with, "I'm glad you mentioned that because this could be the most important day of your life. Many successful people have been in your shoes. If they had let a past experience stand in their way, they never would have made it to where they are today. Would they? (Don't stop.) Since the first time you were ripped off, many opportunities have come your way, haven't they? (Don't stop.) Opportunities that were good for you and your family. You passed them up, and the person who ripped you off the first time ripped you off again when you did not take advantage of those opportunities. You are being ripped off every time you pass up another good opportunity. You see, you are being ripped off every time you pass up a situation that could help you and your family, and you will continue to be ripped off if you let yourself. You are the only one who can stop this. If you do not take advantage of this opportunity now, you are being ripped off once again. It is time to stop this once and for all. After all, your family doesn't deserve to be ripped off again. Do they?"

By planting the seed that other people, successful people, have been in their same shoes helps the clients realize they are not alone. A good close to use after this close, if they are not quite committed, is the Verbal Ben (which was covered in Chapter 12).

I'LL-THINK-IT-OVER CLOSE

When you hear "I'll think it over," it's just a cry for more information. You have to find out what exactly your clients want to think over. It could be something very minor that has not been covered. Let's find out what it is and try to close the sale.

"I'll think it over."

"That's fine. Obviously you would not take your time thinking this over unless you were really interested. Would you? I'm sure that you will give this very careful consideration. Just to clarify my thinking, what part of the program is it that you want to think over? Is it this? Is it that?" (Here you insert questions that relate to your product, company, warranties, and so on.)

What we are doing here is getting down to a specific objection. We have to find out what exactly is stopping our client. It might be one or two things, maybe more. Nothing is going to happen until we find out. Once these objections surface, we can deal with them one at a time and close the sale.

Many sales are made after a prospect says "no" many, many times because people can and will finally agree with you if given more information. You just have to figure out what new information is needed. If you don't have the tenacity to keep trying and digging for this information, your prospect will walk out the door without buying your product. To help your client make a decision, you must continue to probe so you will know what is needed to close the sale.

Here's another example:

"I agree with you and appreciate what you are saying You should think about it. Do not buy this if it is not right for you. However, if it will do the job for you, you should buy it. What exactly do you have to consider?"

By asking this last question, you learn what the customers' objections are that you must address directly. What *exactly* do they have to think about? You will never know if you don't ask the question. It could be a minor consideration that can be handled very easily.

Sometimes people say they have to think it over because they cannot afford your product. If you can finally get to this point, where affordability emerges as the real problem, you can deal with it in many ways. For example, if you are selling a product that can be financed, you can break it down to make it very affordable. Maybe the price of $20,000 is out of the question; however, $2,000 initially and $200 per month is an easy solution to the problem. Your clients might have to think about $20,000, but being able to finance their purchase with a small initial amount and so much per month doesn't require making such a huge decision. They can make these decisions because you discovered the problem (affordability) and solved it with this new information (information about how the purchase can be financed). We will discuss how to break down these money decisions in the next chapter on Money closes.

As a good example of making a purchase affordable, let me tell you about my wife and I furnishing our home. My wife has great taste! She was not buying inexpensive furniture for our lovely home. No way! We were looking for a piece of furniture to go in our family room, and I was astounded at some of the prices. A couple of times I actually choked! She kept saying, "Honey, it will last us our lifetime. It will last us our lifetime," over and over. I thought it better last longer than that with this these prices. However, this very professional interior designer—or should I say, great salesperson—finally told us about a 12 month no-interest plan. She kept explaining that this lovely piece of furniture could be delivered tomorrow without one dime out of my pocket today. My wife could only see the delivery truck in the driveway the next day. Since there was no interest and I didn't even have to write a check that day, we would be crazy not to take it. Guess what? We not only bought that piece, but we also bought some extra items we just had to have, or so my wife said. The bottom line is my decision was based on new information, and we ended up buying more than what we planned. Since then we have bought many other pieces from this same interior designer (or great salesperson).

When a client says they have to think it over, their hesitation might be due to affordability, or it might be something else. You won't know unless you ask questions. When asking these questions, you have to be careful not to upset or irritate your clients. If they get hot under the collar, they will never provide the real reasons to close the sale.

GUT-FEELING CLOSE

This close can be used as a last-ditch effort to see if you have a chance for a sale.

"I can see you are very interested in our program or you would not have spent this much time with me. Correct? It's obvious the benefits of our program would benefit you and your family, and you will give these special consideration. Right? Let me ask you this: on a scale of one to ten, how would you rate our program?"

I can guarantee the answer to this last question, assuming you have given a good presentation and you have set up this close with the first two questions, will be seven or better 95 percent of the time. The first question is asked in order to get a minor commitment. The second question is designed to make the clients agree that your program's benefits are good for them. The third question is to let them think the presentation is over, and now they can leave if they answer in a positive way. Wrong! It is to get the score high for the following:

"In the course of our conversation today we have been talking about the affordability of our program, thinking it over, checking certain things out, and other considerations. The truth is you have thought about it for many years (owning land, a house, investments, insurance, vacations, and so on). It always comes down to one thing that stops us from making these decisions—fear. Fear can keep us from making decisions that can help our future. The tragedy of this is that I can never overcome your fear no matter how hard I try. We have owners with families who have benefited for years by owning our product, thousands of truly happy people. Yet, even if they were all here and they all told you how they have benefited, you would still have that fear. Fear can destroy all the great things we can ever have in our lives. The only way to get over this fear is to start somewhere. Right? (Don't stop.) You see, something is inside us that we have all experienced. It is a gut feeling. You get a feeling in your stomach that says, 'Do it' or 'Don't do it.' The fact is, all your life you have found that your gut feeling is usually right, and when you listen to it, you make a good decision. When you don't listen to it, you wish you had. It happens to all of us. Let's throw out the 'I want to think about it,' the 'I can't afford it,' and everything else. Let me ask you this. What is your gut feeling?"

At times when using this close, your clients will say their gut feeling tells them to go for it. At other times it will bring the final objection or objections to the table. You can handle these objections and close the sale. Again, be very cautious when using this close so you do not get the wrong response. If you use it correctly, you can save many sales.

LET US TALK IT OVER CLOSE

Many products have to be sold with both husband and wife present. If you don't sell both, your cancellation rate will be higher than the national debt. If you give your presentation to just one spouse, you can't expect that spouse to go home and paint the same picture that you could. It won't happen; it can't happen; it never will happen. That one prospect might be higher than a Georgia pine, but 99 percent of the time, a cancellation will occur if one spouse goes home and tries to explain the product to the other.

We discussed cancellations and how to eliminate them in Chapter 6. When working with couples, you have to be aware of certain "deal killers" that can be eliminated if handled properly. When a couple says they want to talk about it for a few minutes, one word or gesture from you can blow the sale.

When the clients ask, "Could you let us talk about it a few minutes?" you respond, "By all means." Then excuse yourself for five minutes, no longer, and come back. If they need more time, they will let you know. When you come back, *always* ask, "Do you have any questions?" *Never* say, "Well, what do you think?" If you do, chances are that is exactly what they are going to do—go home and think about it.

This is a common mistake that blows sales every day. In a day or two they will go shopping around and buy from a real closer, and your money is gone forever. By asking if they have any questions, you can get to the final objection quickly. When they ask to talk about it for a few minutes, chances are they have to discuss only one or two items. When you come back in, you should be down to the last objection or objections. Many times it is not what you say, it is how you say it. Remember that Samson killed thousands of Philistines with the jawbone of an ass, and thousands of sales are lost every day because jawbones say the *wrong* thing at the *right* time. By "right time," I mean closing time.

TAKE AWAY CLOSE

This is the strongest close in the sales profession. When you take something away from a baby, what does it do? It cries, right? The same thing happens when prospects can't have something they want. This is definitely psychological warfare. Something happens in the mind that says, "Don't tell me that. I don't want to hear 'no.'" It wakes up the prospects and makes them listen with complete attention. The clients' will be thinking, "I want that; don't turn me down." The great salesperson acts as if it is not possible to sell it to the client. Customers are so used to hearing "yes! yes! yes!" that when this "no" surfaces, they are thrown completely off base. However, you have to know when to close on the "no" answer. You have to be very careful not to go overboard when using this technique. If clients hear "no" too many times, they will lose interest in your product.

This close should be used when a major objection or concern comes up. When you are selling a product that has lots of bells and whistles, the sentence "No, it doesn't come with that" is very effective. Some products can include extras if they are needed to close the sale. When I bought my last boat, the company gave me a boat cover to close me. These little extras can close a sale faster than anything if used properly.

"Does the boat cover come with the boat?"

"No, the cover is an extra $275."

"That's a shame."

"Where are you going to store your boat?"

"In my garage."

"Then you don't really need one since it won't be out in the open."

"Yeah, but I'd like to have one to keep the dust out."

"That's true. Let me ask you this. If I could throw in the boat cover, would you like to own this boat?"

What we have done here is let the objection sink in with a "no" answer. If we just close after the first question, it doesn't have the same effect. You have to hang the "no" out there for a while to get the full benefit of making him or her want the boat cover even more. Don't close by saying:

"Does the boat cover come with the boat?"

"If it does, do you want it?"

At times this Sharp Angle technique works, but in this situation the "no" is much more effective:

"Do the condominiums come with a boat slip?"

"No."

"What am I supposed to do with my boat when I bring it down?"

"You can use the ramp. Drop it in the water, and pull it out when you are done for the day."

"No way; I need a slip."

"If I could include a slip with the condo, would you like to invest with us?"

This procedure makes your clients want the product more. They are actually buying the added benefit. The product is great, but sometimes the little extras that are thrown in make the difference. Never say, "No problem, we can include that" or "Sure." Take it away, and the closing scene is set.

When selling a product with little extras that can make the sale, we might add them up and present the product at the higher price so we have some leverage. We can always drop the price if the client does not want these extra items. For example:

Boat	$18,000
Trailer	2,500
Cover	275
Skis	200
Rope	50
Vests	200
Total	$21,225

By presenting the full price we have negotiating tools in case they are needed during the offering. Remember, "no" can be the most effective response. Saying "yes," and giving everything away gives us no closing tools. Learn this style, and your sales career will be dramatically enhanced.

I'm Just Looking Close

Many times when we approach a client, their response is "I'm just looking." Let me ask you this question. Why are they on the car lot, in the store, or in your office? Obviously, they have some interest or they wouldn't be there, would they? Of course not.

A great salesperson knows how to turn these lookers into buyers. I've heard all the excuses: "they're just tire kickers," and "they're just wasting my time." These negative responses are what's keeping ordinary salespeople from being great ones. The great salesperson kicks into high gear, and that's why he makes more money. This is when certain trial closes need to be inserted.

For example, here's how to handle "I'm just looking":

"Can I help you?"

"I'm just looking."

"What exactly are you looking for? I would be delighted to help you find it." or "I would be happy to help you save some time."

Once you've said that, you say, "it's right over here." (Turn and start walking. Believe me, they will follow.)

Here's how to respond to "I need to look around":

"I can identify with that. I agree with you. You should look around. How long have you been looking?"

"Just a few days."

Or

"What else have you looked at?"

"A couple of other ones."

"What about their product do you like?" (Wait for an answer.) What about our product do you like?"

These questions bring out the objections that need to be overcome. Remember, the "I'm just looking" response is just a smoke screen in many cases. People put up this brick wall because they don't want to be sold. They feel a salesperson is going to pressure them. By asking these questions, you get to the core so a sale can be made. If you don't ask, somebody is going to make a sale, but it won't be you.

ONLY

CLOSERS

118

make

BIG

MONEY

14

MONEY CLOSES

In many cases the reason we hear excuses such as "I want to think about it," "I never make an instant decision," or "I have to talk to someone" is because money is the real problem. You can assume when you hear these excuses that the problem is money. Because of pride, no one wants to admit that money is the problem. Occasionally you hear, "I can't afford it," but more often you'll hear one of these excuses when the lack of dollars is standing in the way of making a sale.

There are many types of affordability problems. In most situations, the problem is not the total cost of the product. Some products are sold by narrowing in on monthly payments when financing is available, or when only a cash payment plan is available or discounts for cash are offered, the total plan is spread over a two-to-three month period. Some products are sold with lower interest rates based on a higher down payment. Why start at the lowest offer, when by starting at the top we can always come down? You have to start quoting at full price with the highest down payment, highest monthly payment, and shortest term available. By starting at the top, the stage is set for the closing scenario. With some products, people expect to haggle some, or they won't buy. If they don't haggle, they don't feel they got the most for their money. They will then shop around, thinking a better opportunity is elsewhere. If you handle the situation properly, the need to look further stops with your product.

When prospects ask, "Can you finance for a longer period of time?" they are really telling you something pretty basic–the monthly payment is higher than they can fit into their budget. They have told you that if you can overcome this obstacle, you have a sale. If you are selling a product that has a maximum ten-year term and you start at ten years, when and how do you close on this simple question? You don't, my friend.

Let's look at some examples. Suppose you are selling a product that has five-, seven-, or ten-year financing. Say you are starting at the five-year term just as any great salesperson would.

"Mr. and Mrs. Jones, your monthly payment would be $236.12 over five years."

"Do you ever finance for longer than five years?"

"Absolutely. We can go seven years and that would make your payment $202.10, or we could go ten years and your payment would be $174.30." *Wrong!*

This not closing. They have walked into the perfect closing situation, and you blew it. The way a great salesperson would handle this is as follows:

"Mr. and Mrs. Jones, your monthly payment would be $236.12 over five years."

"Do you ever finance for longer than five years?"

"I can appreciate what you are asking. This expense might put a little strain on the budget. Correct? At times we do finance for longer periods. Every situation is different. Let me ask you this, is the monthly payment a little more than you can handle right now?"

"Yes."

"Other than the monthly payment, is there anything else keeping you from owning this product?"

"No."

"What would be comfortable so you could own this and maintain your lifestyle? (Don't stop.) I wouldn't want to change that if I can help you folks." Or you can say, "What would be comfortable without taking any food off your table?" or "What would be an amount you could spend without even thinking about it?" There are many different ways to ask this last question. You can see how to close in this situation. *Never say you can extend the term without asking these questions.* This is the difference between telling and selling.

Another example of this situation is selling products that offer only a cash payment plan without terms. Again, we have to start at the highest offering to set the stage for the close.

"Mr. and Mrs. Jones, the total cost of this product is $10,000."

"How soon would you need the $10,000?"

"Within the next two months." *Wrong!* Never, *ever* say this! They have asked you to close them. By answering this way, you have again lost the chance to close. Answer with "How much time do you need?"

"I'm not sure."

"How much could you come up with today?"

"$2,000."

"Would 30 days be enough time to come up with the balance?"

"We might be able to come up with it by then."

"What if we could set it up so that $4,000 is due in 30 days, and the balance is due in 45 days? Would that work?"

By asking these closing questions, you can make the sale in a short period of time. Giving information without these questions is a definite no-no. The fact is you can be an almanac of information, but your sales career will be over in a hurry.

Money Funnel/T Close

This close is designed to qualify your clients on down payment and monthly payments. Its power is in how you qualify on these two issues. It funnels down to a comfortable down payment and monthly payment.

Many products are sold with different terms based on down payment. Again, sometimes we can give better interest rates and longer terms with bigger down payments. Because of this the close will narrow down the objections until the final one is addressed. If you sell a product with these terms, memorize this close.

Let's say you have a $10,000 product and can take as low as 10 percent down payment over a 10-year period.

$10,000	
Down payment 30%/$3,000.00	Monthly payment $236.12/5 years

Let me walk you through this close step by step.

"John and Mary, the total cost of this product is $10,000. The down payment will be 30 percent or $3,000. Your monthly payment will be $236.12." At this point you might get a money objection. If you hear an objection such as, "We could never come up with $3,000 right now," go right to the down payment problem. If they say, "That monthly payment is out of our budget," go right to the monthly payment. If they don't object to anything, continue with:

"Would $3,000 be comfortable for you?"

"That would be too much at this time."

"I can appreciate what you are saying. How long would it take you to come up with the $3,000?"

"It would take two or three months anyway."

"How much could you come up with today?"

"$500."

"So, $500 today. Could you come up with another $500 in 30 days?"

"Yes, we could probably do that."

"Then the balance of $2,000 over the next couple of months, right?"

The balance of $2,000 isn't important because you have already handled the minimum requirement of $1,000. However, we still need to get this commitment to strengthen the final close. We have now funneled down and handled the down payment, but we still have to deal with the monthly payment. Go to the monthly payment column and continue with:

"How about the $236.12? Would that work for you?"

"Well, that's a little high for us right now."

"I understand completely. What would be comfortable for you without taking any food off the table?"

"$200 would work."

The following is an example of how it would look to a client on paper:

$10,000

Down Payment	Monthly Payment
$3,000	$236.12/5 years
2-3 months	$200
$500 today	
$500 30 days	
$2,000 2 months	

Everything is written down on paper so your client can see what has been agreed upon. In this example, we can go as low as $1,000 down. We got a commitment on the $1,000 over 30 days. Knowing we can go as long as a 10-year term, we then get a commitment on the monthly payment.

You should know what these monthly payments are based on—5, 7, or 10 years—so you will know where you are going. This close can be used on many different products. Again, if it can be used with your product, memorize it. It will make you a tremendous amount of money.

Implement Objection Closing

Sometimes we have to read our clients' thoughts. We can be tipped off to what the problems might be by observing their body language. We talked about these signals earlier in the book:

Crossing legs with hands on chin

Leaning back in chair with arms crossed

Legs shaking up and down (indicates nervousness)

Not making eye contact

Not sitting down

Head shaking sideways

By observing your prospect, you might see these red flags. If and when they do appear, you have to realize a problem exists for you to solve. Sometimes you have to go through a mental process back to a question or objection that came up during your presentation. However, money will generally be the main objection with most products. People do not want to part with their hard-earned cash. If you don't ask clients what the problem is, they will walk away from your offer, and you will never know for certain why they did not buy your product.

"It is obvious that you would like to invest in our product, but right now the initial investment isn't comfortable for you. Right?"

"At the present time this product is something you would like to own, but the total cost is a little uncomfortable. Correct?"

"You can see that this product would save you money in the long run, but I can see that the monthly payment is not comfortable for you. Isn't that true?"

"You can see how you and your family would benefit by owning this product, but I can also see you were not planning to spend this much. Right?"

"It is apparent you would like to own the product if we could work out the financing. Correct?"

"You can see how this product would increase the sales of your company, but right now this much money might not be in the budget. Right?"

By asking these questions, we find out what the problem is and can overcome the objection.

"It is obvious that you would like to invest in our product, but right now the initial investment isn't comfortable for you. Right?"

"That's right."

"How long would it take to come up with it?" Or "What would be comfortable for you at this time?" Or "How much of it could you come up with now?"

"At the present time this product is something you would like to own, but the total cost of it is a little uncomfortable. Correct?"

"Yes."

"How much of a deposit could you leave today?" Or "How much were you planning to spend?" Or "How much did you think it would cost?"

"You can see this product would save you money in the long run, but I can also see that the monthly payment is not comfortable for you. Isn't that true?"

"That's true."

"How much could you handle on a monthly basis?" Or "What would be comfortable without taking any food off the table?" Or "How much could you save per month to own this product in the future?"

"You can see how you and your family would benefit by owning this product, but I can also see that you weren't planning to spend this much. Right?"

"Right."

"What would be comfortable at this time?" Or "How much does the budget allow?" Or "How much too much is it?"

There are many ways to ask the questions. Depending on your product, ask questions that would help you close the sale. If a prospect says "no" to any of these money questions, follow up with one simple question, "What exactly is it?" This will bring the objection out so you can overcome it.

By asking this question, "How much could you save per month to own this product in the future?" I'm *not* trying to find out when in the future this prospect can buy the merchandise. I am trying to qualify on a monthly payment if financing is available. If our prospect can save $50 per month to own our product in the future, and I have financing that will fit this dollar amount, I've got a sale today. At times when the amount of money is definitely out of the question, you have to explain how a less expensive product might fit the client's needs at the present time. If you have a trade-up policy, this could be an excellent way to handle the money problem.

The Implement Objection close is excellent to use on the "Yeah! Yeah!" clients we discussed in Chapter 9. When people have asked no questions or have no objections, these money implementations can turn the Yeah! Yeah! prospect around. If the client doesn't ask any questions or make any objections, you won't make a sale. By asking these questions, if money is not a problem, you bring out objections so you can address them and close the sale. However, in most cases, money will be the problem.

TALK TO SOMEONE CLOSE

This is one of the excuses we hear on an ongoing basis. In most cases, having to talk to someone is not an objection. Something in our prospect's mind is telling them not to go forward with a decision to buy our product. We could have left something out of our presentation, or they might be questioning our credibility. But money is probably the actual reason. We have to conquer and divide to find the real objection. By using this close we can get down to the actual reason for not buying the product. Remember that pride and ego are strong walls that have to be knocked down. Because of their pride, our prospects will not volunteer this information. We have to have the intestinal fortitude to help these people. It can be done in a very empathetic way. It has to be done gently by putting ourselves on the prospects' level so they don't feel embarrassed.

The following is a form of intimidation that is totally unnecessary:

"Well, I guess you can't afford it."

"It's a shame you don't have the money."

"You need to come back when you are in a better situation."

"This is not for you."

"Borrow the money somewhere."

Great salespeople know how to use the velvet hammer approach. I do not understand why certain salespeople think total intimidation is the way to sell. I agree that intimidation has to be used at particular times but not very often. When the intimidating style is used, it can come off as obnoxious pressure that can irritate your clients. This macho approach will lose you more sales than any one thing in the profession.

The following are examples that have the right appeal when used in closing:

"I'd like to talk to my father."

"I can see that he won't be making the decision for you. But at certain times we need a little financial help, and it's nice to have someone who can help us. Right? (Don't stop.) Don't get me wrong. The reason I asked is that you probably need help with the down payment. Right now I would have a tough time coming up with this much money, too. (Put yourself on their level.) Is this the problem?" (Point to the paper where the down payment is written.)

Or

"That's natural. I agree with you. You should talk to someone. There's a lot to toss around. Who do you have to talk to?"

"My dad."

"What exactly do you need to discuss with him?"

Again, this last question brings out the objection. Once you know what the objection really is, you can close. If you don't uncover the objection, it will stay hidden, and a sale could be lost.

"I'd like to discuss this with my uncle."

"It's obvious he won't be making the decision for you. However, when we need a little help dollar-wise, it's nice to be able to confide in someone. Correct? (Don't stop.) I've had to do the same thing in the past. But to be able to do this on your own would make you feel a lot better. Wouldn't it? (This question is an ego builder. Don't stop.) If it were an amount you could handle yourself without going to someone else, you wouldn't need to talk to your uncle. Would you?"

"No."

"How much could you handle without having to borrow anything?"

Once you get the money commitment, you can work out the situation. Without your knowing what the real objection is, nothing can happen except another lost soul walking out not owning your product.

The flow of this close is what makes it forceful. By listening to the excuse you can infer what the actual reason might be, which is probably money. By empathizing you get on the same level as your client, building trust. By solving the clients' problems without their having to borrow the money, you put yourself on their level and build their egos. By asking if it was an amount they could handle so they wouldn't have to talk to someone, you conquer the excuse. The final closing question determines what this amount is.

The key to this close is to assume that money is the problem. Chances are they are not going to talk to someone. If they actually did, the person they talk to is going to blow your sale. This person knows little if anything about your product and probably doesn't want to loan the money. If money isn't what's keeping them from buying your product, your clients will tell you, and you can ask what is keeping them from going ahead with the purchase. Once they explain it, you can close on the real objection or objections.

BONUS CLOSE

It is common for sales organizations to run incentive programs for increasing production. These programs are very beneficial and help to motivate managers and salespeople alike. Cash rewards, trips, and gifts are a few of the incentives that are offered. These incentives can also become great closing tools. Very few typical salespeople ever take advantage of these tools. Used as third-party stories with Sharp Angle closes, these rewards can justify longer terms, lower down payments, and better interest rates. When coming down the money funnel (the Money Funnel/T close), you should have a good reason for better financing. If a bonus program is taking place, it is an excellent justification. After coming down to a comfortable amount that is agreed upon (for example, a total of $10,000 with a $3000 down payment–$500 today, $500 in 30 days, and $2000 in 2 months with a $200 per month payment), follow with the Bonus close.

"The president of our company told my manager if a certain number of people got involved with us, he would give the manager and his wife a one-week trip to the Caribbean, all expenses paid. My manager is very motivated because his wife really wants to take that trip! She already has her bags packed. She calls three or four times a day to see how we are doing. He's going to have to take her whether the company pays for it or he pays for it himself. So right now is a good time to see if this can be worked out. If we can do this (point back to the money), would you like to get involved today?" Now listen, and wait for an answer. If the clients say "yes," you obviously have a sale. If they say "no," ask what is standing in their way. To get down to an amount agreed upon and to not explain why this can be done can make the clients think it's too good to be true. This again can cause cancellations and lost credibility. Using the bonus as a third-party story sets up the final Sharp Angle closing questions: "If we can do this, would you get involved today?"

Many third-party stories can be used. If a bonus program is in place, use it to your advantage; use something else if there is not a bonus program.

CREDIT CLOSE

This close can also be used as a justifying reason to work out the money when using the Money Funnel/T close.

"If we could get you involved like this, $500 today, $500 in 30 days, $2000 in 2 months, and $200 per month would you like to own this product?"

"Yes."

"Do you have good credit?"

"Yes."

"How good?" Or "Do you know your rating?" Or "Are you ever late on any payments?"

Any of these questions can be used. People like to tell other people how good their credit is. By asking them, you can justify why certain things such as better financing can be obtained. In many instances good credit will give people a chance at better terms. I've seen second homes sold with down payments from 10 to 25 percent and with better interest rates depending on the credit risk. Automobiles can also be obtained with better interest rates if one's credit is good. If your product can be sold like this, use the credit close.

SALE WAS ON CLOSE

All merchandise goes on sale from time to time. Sales are designed to get more prospects coming through your doors on specific days. When the sale is over, many items are left at discount prices. Out-of-style inventory, older models, and year-end-clearances are a few examples. You should always know which inventory can be sold at discounted prices. If, and only if, these items can truly be sold at sale prices should the Sale Was On close be used. Maybe the merchandise is off display and stocked back in the warehouse.

Did you see all the advertising we did last week for our sale?

Did you come in last week for our sale?

Did you know about the sale we had last week?

You should have come in last week; we had a big sale.

By asking one of these questions or in some way conveying to your prospect that a sale was on but is now over creates the feeling that the client missed out on saving some money. However, if you have stock that can be sold at the same sale price, your prospect can still save that money, and you are doing him or her a tremendous favor. Follow one of the previous questions with:

"I can check to see if you can have it for the same price. Would this interest you?" You ask this closing question after you can see that your prospect is interested. By using the close this way, you are being completely honest with your customer. Your product was on sale during the promotion. However, instead of just blurting out that it can be purchased for the same sale dollars, you are asking a closing question. In addition, a sense of urgency to act now has been instilled. A sale today is much better than trying to get the sale tomorrow. (Close the sale *today*.)

I NEVER MAKE AN INSTANT DECISION CLOSE

People generally don't like to make instant decisions. If you have done your job building value, creating need and desire, and generating urgency, people will move to purchase your product. "I never make an instant decision" goes hand in hand with "I want to think about it," "I have to talk to someone," and the rest of the excuses we hear. This excuse again is generally about money. But it might not be the total cost. If financing is presented, it is usually the down payment or the monthly payment, not the total cost, that is the problem. Here is the "I never make an instant decision" close:

"I never make an instant decision."

"I agree with you completely. I'd have to consider $3000 and $236.12 per month, too. (Don't mention the total cost.)

Which of these would keep you from getting involved, the $3000 or the $236.12 per month?"

"BOTH."

Then you concentrate on both the down payment and monthly payment. If it is just the down payment, go to that figure; if it is the monthly payment, concentrate on that figure. After going to the problem, confirm that the other figure is okay. If money is not the problem, ask what is, and handle that objection.

Another way to deal with this objection is with complete urgency. "I never make an instant decision" is another way of saying "I want to think about it." The following is designed to motivate the client to make an immediate decision. When working on the money, use this approach:

"I never make an instant decision."

"I agree with you completely. I'd have to consider $3000 and $236.12 per month, too. (Don't mention total cost.) Which one would be the problem?"

"I couldn't handle the $236.12 per month at the present time."

"How much would be easy to handle without even having to think about it? (Snap your fingers.) How much?"

I guarantee you will get an amount right away. When the client answers, the thinking is all over. Try it—you'll be amazed!

One day, a good friend of mine, called me from Denver, Colorado. He and his manager were having problems getting people to make decisions to buy their product. They asked me what I would recommend. I explained this close to them and had the manager write it down. He repeated it to me. I explained the close only worked if you snap your fingers, immediately followed by asking "How much?" The next day I got a call from the manager, and he couldn't thank me enough. He tried it and found it worked perfectly. The mind is very powerful. In this close, we are programming the mind to do and say what we want. Once the mind is programmed, the amount will come out automatically. Once you know this figure, you know what you have to work with. Turn out the lights; the decision has been made.

I Can't Afford It/It Costs Too Much Close

When we hear this, clients are telling us something we can deal with head on. But what are they telling us? What can they not afford? The total cost? The down payment? The monthly payment? Maybe all of these. We have to isolate each one to be sure, but before we isolate each one we want to make sure affordability is the only objection left. Always deal with the other objections first to make sure they are sold.

"I can't afford it."

"Is it the down payment or the monthly payment?"

"Both."

"It is obvious that you would like to invest in our product if it were affordable. Right?"

"Yes."

"Other than the money involved, is there anything else standing in your way from getting involved with us?"

"No."

"I can't afford it."

"Is it the down payment or the monthly payment?"

"Monthly payment."

"Other than the monthly payment is there anything else standing in your way of getting involved with us?"

"No."

"I can't afford it."

"What part can't you afford?"

"Down payment."

"Other than the down payment, is there anything else standing in your way of getting involved with us?"

"No."

If nothing else is in the way, close with:

"If we could make it affordable, would you like to own it?" All these different types of questions close on the response of your client. If it is affordability, narrow in on it, and close the sale.

Another way of handling this objection is as follows:

"I agree with you and totally understand. You need to consider your finances. If you can't afford it, you shouldn't buy it. However, if there's any possible way we can make it affordable, you should buy it. If it were affordable, you would obviously take advantage of it, wouldn't you?"

"Yes."

"Is it the initial investment or the monthly investment that you're worried about?"

If a customer says she can't afford it, that doesn't mean she *can't* afford it *if* the financing is worked out. You have to break down the objection to get to the real problem. In most cases, a money obstacle can be worked out if you offer other financial solutions. The customer isn't telling us she doesn't want the product. Again, she needs more information. If she says it is not the initial investment or the monthly investment, but the total cost, you have to dig a little more.

Here's a conversation in which the customer offers an objection, and I provide the understanding response that handles the objection:

"The whole thing costs too much."

"How long have you considered owning one?"

"Quite a while."

"How much did you plan on spending?" or "How much did you think it would cost?"

This last question brings out the dollar amount the customer has to spend. The response can also tell you if he has looked at your competition. If so, you have to defend the cost of your product by building its value. If he says he could buy the product for less elsewhere, you need to find out if it is the same exact product as the one he is looking at with you.

These Money closes are used to get to the clients' real objections. By using these closes we get down to the core of the problem. We have to get to this point to see if our prospects' objections are real or if they're a smoke screen for some other objection. Many different questions can be used in these closes. Plug in your product, and see which ones will work for you. Remember, only closers make big money.

In this chapter we have gone over different objections. We sometimes use the same questions in response to these objections because repetition can be powerful. If you will go over and over these questions and practice them so they become part of your subconscious mind, you will become a great closer. You can become so mentally trained you will spit them out like a machine.

I am giving you the tools; now it is up to you to use them. If you will memorize them, you will make more money in a very short period of time. Stop explaining your product, and start closing.

15

IN SUMMARY

As I said at the beginning of this book, sales is a high paying profession for those individuals who are willing to do what it takes to be a great salesperson. Let's take a look at what you can do to be a successful salesperson. These are high points that are covered in earlier chapters.

Remember, there is no substitute for positive thinking and self-motivation. You have to be willing to take the time to read books, listen to tapes, go to sales seminars, and rehearse tie-downs. Don't just go through the motions and hope you will sell something. Do not take short cuts. Challenge yourself mentally. When you experience discouragement, remember the story about the gold miner, and don't be a quitter. Keep in mind that you may have to spend money to make money: a truly great salesperson has so much confidence in his abilities, he's willing to spend his own money to generate sales.

You can learn from anyone, not just successful salespeople. Don't judge people by the clothes they wear or the cars they drive. Qualify your clients by asking questions about their jobs, their families, and

ONLY CLOSERS

137

make BIG MONEY

so on. Then determine what they can afford, take control of the situation, and lead your clients to a product that is appropriate for their income level.

You have to make a friend before you can make a sale. Your customers have to trust you before they will make a decision to spend their money on your product. Use the warmup to establish trust. Do not start your presentation until your clients are warmed up. Then be able to adjust your presentation to any situation that comes up or any kind of personality you encounter. Always keep your commitments. When you agree to do something, you must follow through.

Learn how to apply pressure by pulling at the client's heart strings. Memorize a number of third-party stories that you can tell. Relate your client's situation to someone else's so they don't feel pressured or threatened. You can use a third-party story not only to explain the warranty of your product, but also to cover its important points.

Remember to keep it simple! Most people get confused if more than two or three issues are involved. Some products have so many good qualities, salespeople often oversell them. Although value will always justify the price, too much value can be too good to be true.

Your presentation should establish the credibility of your company. People want to know that your company is going to be around to service their accounts and take care of any problems that might arise in the future.

Value justifies a purchase. It can overcome the cost of any product. If the customer believes the product has value, the dollar amount, as long as it isn't totally out of line, is generally not important.

Don't downgrade the competition. Doing so drives the customer away. Agree with clients when they praise the competition. Say something like "they have a good product," or "they do a good job." By saying this, you are implying that you are not afraid of another product, and your client feels the honesty of the salesperson. By pointing out the positive values of your product, you can eliminate your competition without downgrading them.

Listen to your clients! Let them tell you how and when to close. Sales is 70 to 80 percent listening and 20 to 30 percent selling. Watch your clients' body language, and learn what different postures and gestures mean. By watching body language, you'll learn when and where to go with your presentation.

Know the information in your presentation book like the back of your hand, and keep it clean and up to date. You can use a presentation book to keep your prospects' attention focused on what you are saying.

Downselling is the act of directing customers to the product we have decided they should own because they might not be able to afford what they want. Read Chapter 5, and learn the art of downselling.

Never sell on rescission! If you think a client may want to cancel after you've made the sale, stop and go over the good points of the product. Talk to the client to draw out his reservations, and then address them to make a solid sale. Remember, people buy some products strictly because they're excited about them, without using any logic, but after the excitement has faded, they have to be able to logically defend their purchase. It's up to you to go over the logical reasons why buying your product is a good idea. When a cancellation occurs, don't let it defeat you. You have to take the good with the bad. Challenge yourself to go out and make a sale.

Don't be afraid of the word "no." Remember, the more NOs you hear, the closer you are to a YES. Be familiar with the most common objections to buying your product. They'll be some versions of the following:

I never make an instant decision.

I can't afford it.

I want to think about it.

I have to talk to someone.

I'm just looking.

When you become familiar with these objections, drop seeds to eliminate them before they come up. If you wait until the client verbalizes them, it might be too late. Use tie-downs to get minor commitments needed in order to make the sale.

When you make a statement about the product you're selling, follow it with a tie-down, such as "don't you agree?" Use positive statements such as "It's clear to people like yourselves who work hard for their money that you deserve to drive a luxury car like this. Isn't it?" Get as many YESes as possible during your presentation. Memorize and rehearse your tie-downs so they become a natural part of your presentation. Use different ones to avoid giving a presentation that sounds canned.

Don't be afraid of your client's objections because they reveal the information you need to know in order to close. Learn the art of handling objections (see Chapter 8). Conquer your client's excuses with empathetic statements and questions. Ask questions that will keep your client involved in what you're saying. Learn the various Sharp Angle closes (see Chapter 10), and use them, but remember that your timing is crucial when you use these closes. Use the Time Machine and Past, Present, and Future closes to keep your clients from making mistakes that they'll regret later. Remember, people need your help in making decisions. People are so afraid of making a bad decision, they won't make any decision at all. It is your duty to help these people, or they will end up with nothing. If you are selling a good product, your clients will be grateful that you helped them with these decisions.

Here are tips to help you with successful closings:

1. Agree and empathize.

2. Because of the fear of buying, buyers are not always truthful. Try to get to the truth.

3. When working with couples, the wife makes the decision 90 to 95 percent of the time. Get next to her, and make your job easier.

4. Lead the customer to find the final objection.

5. Know the objections that are going to come up. Be prepared to overcome them. (All products have four or five.)

6. Use the power of emotion to close. (Use dreams and children; tug at the heart strings.) It's difficult to do, but you will feel more comfortable as you do it more often.

7. Use change of pace techniques. When clients are tense, ask them a question about anything other than the product. Make them feel at ease. Then strike with a closing question. Go for the jugular vein.

8. Don't talk past the close.

9. Make the client understand the product before the close. This creates the value needed to close.

10. Realize that money is the real objection 95 percent of the time.

11. Ask a closing question; then shut up.

12. Let facial expressions tell you when to close.

13. Intimidate if necessary.

14. When the opportunity to close comes—strike!

15. "I want to think about it" is a cry for more information. Don't listen to it, or you will be ruined.

16. *You* make the decision for the customer.

17. Use the information given to you by the client earlier in the presentation to close. Good closers listen, listen, listen.

18. Once the sale has been made, talk about anything but the product while you're filling out the paperwork.

19. Blame yourself for not qualifying the clients properly if their credit is turned down.

20. Use tie-downs for a powerful close.

21. Make friends before making the sale.

22. Take control.

23. Qualify. Don't prejudge.

Finally, I would like to make a statement my wife, Jody, told me one day. Yesterday is the past, tomorrow is the future. Today is a gift. Maybe that's why they call it "the present." Today you have a choice. To continue your old ways or start new. Memorize, and use this material. Read it, highlight it, and read it again. It will increase your sales, which in turn will increase your income. You and your family definitely deserve it. Don't you agree?

GLOSSARY: THE GREAT SALESPERSON'S VOCABULARY

cancellations: By helping the client defend his purchase with logic, you can reduce the chance of cancellations. See also *rescissions*.

children: Use children to tug at your clients' heartstrings. When selling to a family that includes children, address leading questions to the kids, who can and will put pressure on their parents.

closer: A great salesperson is a closer. She knows when to close and how to close. She becomes familiar with the various closes covered in this book and knows which ones should be used in various situations.

closing: Learn the science of closing because closing is what matters in the sales profession. No matter how polished your presentation is, it's all for naught if it doesn't lead to a close.

competition: Never downgrade the competition. Instead, build value in your product and build credibility in you and your company.

control: A great salesperson takes control of the conversation with his clients. He leads them to buy what he has decided they can afford.

credibility: A great salesperson builds credibility in herself, her company, and her product.

decisions: People need help making decisions. That's where the great salesperson comes in. A great salesperson helps customers to reach a decision by helping them realize that just because they've made a bad decision in the past, that's no reason not to make a sound decision now.

desire: You must have the desire to succeed and to improve your standard of living if you want to be a great salesperson.

empathy: Use empathy, not sympathy, to put yourself on the same level as your customers. It shows your customers that you understand them.

ONLY CLOSERS make BIG MONEY

143

enthusiasm:	Enthusiasm is contagious. A great salesperson gets the customers excited about his product.
if:	This is the biggest word in the salesperson's vocabulary: *If* I could, would you? Would you, *if* I could? Use *if*, *if*, and *if* some more.
information:	When clients say, "I want to think about it," that's just an excuse. They need more information from you so you can close the sale.
listen:	Making sales is 70 to 80 percent listening and 20 to 30 percent selling.
logic:	Customers often buy a product when they become excited about it. Building enthusiasm for your product is important, but remember that the customer must be able to defend her purchase with logic.
mental:	A great salesperson gets into the customer's minds by planting seeds that address objections even before they've been brought up. A great salesperson must be mentally tough.
motivate:	Do what it takes to stay motivated! Read books, listen to tapes, psyche yourself up so you can motivate your customers.
negativity:	This is a cancer that can ruin your career (and your life). A great salesperson has a positive outlook and avoids negative people.
no:	The word *no* is a good word. When a salesperson says "no," it makes his clients want his product even more. The more NOs you hear during your presentation, the closer you are to hearing a YES.
objections:	The only objections you have to fear are those that are unspoken. A great salesperson is glad to hear objections because he can respond to them. You have to listen and ask questions to bring the customer's objections into the open.
obvious:	This is a positive word that you can use to get agreement from your customers: "It's *obvious* you like our product, right?" "Obviously, you would *if* I could, wouldn't you?"
opportunity:	Instead of saying "it's a good deal," use the word *opportunity*: "it's a great opportunity. The word *deal* has negative connotations (from Tom Hopkins).

ONLY CLOSERS

144

make

BIG

MONEY

past:	The past is gone; tomorrow isn't here yet. The only thing you can do anything about is what's happening right now (from Mark J. McDonnell).
positive:	A great salesperson does what it takes to stay positive.
prejudge:	Never prejudge, always qualify your customers to find out what product they can afford.
presentation:	An effective presentation is simple, and it builds credibility in you and your organization, value in your product, and enthusiasm in your customers.
pressure:	A great salesperson applies subtle pressure, using the velvet hammer approach (which means the client never realizes pressure has been applied).
qualify:	Never prejudge, always qualify your customers.
questions:	Ask your clients questions to lead them to the close.
quit:	This word is not part of the great salesperson's vocabulary.
red flag:	Observe your client's body language to detect signs of resistance. For example, when a client crosses his arms in front of his chest, that's a red flag that your presentation is not being received favorably.
rescissions:	Never sell on rescission.
seeds:	Plant seeds in the customer's mind to harvest a sale. You can plant seeds to eliminate objections on the front end so you can close on the back end.
third-party stories:	Tell third-party stories. Customers often buy the story—and then the product.
tie-down:	This is a trial closing technique used to get YESs throughout the presentation so you can close. Memorize the tie-downs in this book so you can sound natural when you use them.
trust:	You must make a friend before you make a sale. Use the warmup to establish trust so the client knows he's dealing with an honest person.
value:	Build value in the product. Price is not an obstacle if the client believes in the value of the product.
warmup:	Use the warmup to establish trust. You must make a friend before you can make a sale.

ONLY CLOSERS 145 make BIG MONEY

Book Order Form

Please send me _____ copies of "Only Closers Make Big Money" at $14.95 per copy. Add $3.95 per book to cover postage and handling. Texas residents add 8% sales tax.

Name:_____

Address:_____

City, State Zip:_____

Make check or money order payble to:

Historical Publications
8030 North Mo-Pac Suite #305
Austin, Texas 78759

Total Book order: $_____
Texas residents, 8% sales tax $_____
Shipping/Handling (3.95 each) $_____

Total amount enclosed: $_____

For your convenience, we also accept MasterCard, Visa, or you can call our Toll-Free number:

1-800-880-6789

www.historicalpublications.com

closers@historicalpublications.com